Increasing Your Wealth in Good Times and Bad

Specific guidelines for an investment strategy that works,
plus investment analysis programs
you can run on your own microcomputer.

**by
Eugene M. Lerner
and
Richard M. Koff**

Probus Publishing Company
118 North Clinton
Chicago, IL 60606

This publication is designed to provide accurate and authorita-
tive information in regard to the subject matter covered. It is
sold with the understanding that the publisher is not engaged
in rendering legal, accounting or other professional service. If
legal advice or other expert assistance is required, the services
of a competent professional person should be sought.

FROM A DECLARATION OF PRINCIPLES JOINTLY ADOPTED
BY A COMMITTEE OF THE AMERICAN BAR ASSOCIATION
AND A COMMITTEE OF PUBLISHERS.

Library of Congress Cataloging in Publication Data

Lerner, Gene.
    Increasing your wealth in good times and bad.

    Includes index.
    1. Investments—Handbooks, manuals, etc.
I. Koff, Richard M.   II. Title.
HB4527.L47 1985   332.6'78   84–24928
ISBN 0–917253–06–X

Library of Congress Catalog Card No. 84–24928

Printed in the United States of America

1 2 3 4 5 6 7 8 9 0

Preface

You probably don't think of yourself as wealthy. But whether you have a couple of hundred dollars tucked away in the kitchen cookie jar, or a couple of hundred thousand in a savings account, that accumulation *is* your wealth and there are safe and reliable ways to make it grow, no matter who is in the White House or what the Dow Jones is doing.

We are *not* going to tell you how to turn your two hundred dollars into a million by investing in real estate or deep sea salvage or rare jewels. Our experience is that these schemes have about as much chance of working as you have of winning a million-dollar lottery. *Somebody* wins, it's true, but somehow it never turns out to be you.

We are going to show you that with very little effort you can preserve your wealth and make it grow at a rate that, over the long term, is as good as if not better than that achieved by all but the most successful speculators. There is nothing magical or complicated in our method: It will take into account your tolerance for risk, your age, family situation, anticipated needs for cash, and the current stage of the business cycle.

Today there is a bewildering variety of very complicated ways you can invest your money. You may have noticed that when a "financial planner" (meaning salesperson) explains one to you, you will understand it only long enough to write the check. Instead we will concentrate on the three main categories of investment, explain the basic principles of how each works, and show you how to divide your savings among the three.

We will also give you the tools you need to choose

specific stocks or options, bonds, or money market instruments. These tools include guidelines to help you evaluate the performance of individual stocks, bonds and money market instruments. If you don't like doing arithmetic by hand we provide computer programs that will do much of the number crunching for you.

Despite all this talk of computer programs and analytical techniques, we think that you, the investor, are more important than the numbers. Thus, we include six chapters devoted to typical individuals or couples and our recommendations for their investment decisions. Throughout the book we repeatedly refer to real people having to cope with real life situations. Because in the last analysis wealth demonstrates its value only when it is used — used to buy a new home, provide a safe retirement, pass along to your grandchildren. If we have helped you buy a better home or a safer retirement we will have accomplished our purpose.

Eugene Lerner
Richard Koff

Contents

Chapter 1

The Myth of the Sure Thing

Did you ever lose money in the stock market? Welcome to the club — so did we. But are you a chronic loser? Do three investments out of four barely keep pace with inflation? If so, your investment strategy can benefit from some expert attention.

Consider the way most people handle their life savings. George Stevens (not his real name), bought a stock for $10.50 a share late last year and, at one time, it traded up to 19⅞. But George had set a target price of $20 and so when it receded from the high, he stuck with it — and rode it down to $8.25 before, disgusted, he sold at a loss of more than $2 a share.

We are not suggesting that we can tell you exactly when a high has been reached, but we do feel that when a price slides more than 20 percent off the high, it is probably a good time to sell — no matter how much profit you don't get to enjoy.

Or look at Jack Jones (an equally fictitious name) who heard — in strictest confidence — about a company that was about to announce a new technological breakthrough that would revolutionize a whole category of consumer products. Clearly this meant to Jones that the stock price was going to leap whole mountains at a single bound. He bought the stock with every penny he had tucked away and in due course the company did make an announcement. It *was* a new product, and it *was* innovative, but the stock price just sat there, and after a few days it actually began to fall. Jones held on until finally it became apparent that he had bought at the top of the market. Jones' "inside" information had to have been known by hundreds of other investors who, if anything, had the information well before Jones did and had run up the price of the stock long before Jones' buy order reached his broker.

Better yet, consider Harriet Brown (fictional lady). Brown prided herself on looking at the fundamentals. She read the *Wall Street Journal, Business Week,* and *Scientific American* and she decided that genetic engineering was the coming hot new technology. Her broker gave her the names of three companies that had divisions exploring genetic engineering products. She sold her shares in IBM and invested it all in one of the companies. A year later the stock was still drifting around the same price. Profits from the contract the company won from the federal government were more than offset by losses in another division of the company.

Brown's error was more subtle than the two earlier examples, but just as fatal. She had not examined the relationship between the stock price and the underlying value of the entire company. In this case the best that could have happened is that the company would, indeed, have succeeded in the genetic engineering field and the stock would, eventually, come to be worth what she paid for it.

No one knows for sure whether a particular stock will go up in price after he buys it any more than a professional baseball player knows for sure that he will get a hit the next time he is at bat. What he does know is the odds — that if he follows a regimen of practice and study he'll get his share of hits.

Or take a look at the gambling casinos. Those Las Vegas hotels don't know for sure which bettor will win at each turn of the roulette wheel or each throw of the dice. They do know that a thousand bets will leave a predictable percentage with the house — predictable enough to support a large payroll, thick carpets, free drinks for customers, taxes, and a handsome profit for the owners.

The two major determinants of investment strategy are *risk* and *return.* Your objective is simply to get the most return for what you consider a tolerable risk.

Not everyone has the same tolerance for risk. A retired person has a very different tolerance than that of a young person starting on a new career. Nor does everyone have the same need for current income. An executive with a high salary will be less dependent on income from a portfolio than a unemployed single woman supporting young children.

In spite of these differences, there are three rules that apply to all:

Three Rules for Basic Investment

1.   You reduce your risk by diversifying your investments. You should hold all three major categories of financial instruments — stocks (also called equities), bonds, and money market instruments. And you should hold more than one or two different stocks — we recommend that you hold at least 10 and preferably as many as 25 or 30. Diversification limits the inevitable random variations that are out there waiting to pounce on you. It is the most effective way to keep the odds on your side.

2.   You increase return by designing an investment strategy that responds to changes in the business cycle. This means that there will be times when your portfolio has a large percentage of stocks and others when it has a large percentage in money market instruments or bonds. The proportions will be based on your personal needs for income and current and predictable trends in prices and interest rates.

3.   You consistently select stocks, bonds, or money market instruments following a plan that raises the odds that you will do well and reduces the odds that you will sustain losses. This is not as difficult as it seems if you act on a set of principles that are discussed in later chapters.

The reasoning behind these three rules is straightforward. Most stock prices move in concert most of the time. When the market as a whole rises, most stock prices go up; when the market falls it is difficult to find and own those which move counter to the prevailing trend and continue to rise. Since the prices of stocks tend to move together, it is better to be fully invested in stocks during some periods and only partially invested during others.

But while stock prices tend to move together, they do not all move by the same amount. Some will experience a large percentage change; others a much smaller amount. It is statistically safer, therefore, to invest in many different stocks so that the poorer performers will be balanced by the winners. Certainly your returns would be better if you could pick only the winners, but there is no system we have seen that consistently does that. There are many systems that promise to improve your odds of picking winners—some suggest that you concentrate on small, emerging growth companies, others that you should stick to the technological leaders, still others say you should buy only companies that have continually improving earnings but are relatively inexpensive in terms of their underlying assets. But none of these weeds out *all* the losers and if you were unlucky enough to put all your money into a loser you could easily face a disaster far more devastating than the small amount of lost returns that a diversified portfolio would provide.

There is nothing magical or particularly complicated in the creation of an investment strategy that follows our three rules. They have been used by institutional investors and fund managers for years. The difference is that now, for the first time, we have small computers to do the kind of detail work that only large investors could previously afford.

We'll list sources of data necessary to these analyses and provide a few short, but helpful, computer programs that simplify the number crunching (Appendices C, D, E). You may copy the programs and adapt them to your computer yourself or you may want to buy the compiled version in disk form, which includes the listed programs plus a number of more sophisticated ones tailored to your hardware. (For additional information about this item, refer to the card inserted in the back of this book.)

In short, we will help you be as organized and logical about your investments as you are about your business or profession, without taking an inordinate amount of your time or attention.

Chapter 2

Instruments that Make a Portfolio

An investment portfolio is best thought of as a mixture of three major categories of financial instruments—short-term securities (such as Treasury Bills); long-term, fixed-income securities (bonds); and common stocks (equities). There are many other ways to invest, among them, options, and futures contracts. You may also consider physical assets such as paintings, gold, diamonds, antiques, real estate, and so forth. These can give their owners a warm feeling of possession, and they may even increase in value, however, their prices depend on a number of additional factors which make them more difficult to manage and, with the exception of a home, inappropriate as investments for many of us.

The three instruments with which we will be most concerned are short-term money market instruments, long-term bonds, and common stocks. These all share two important properties: Their prices are readily available, and they are liquid, i.e., they can be sold quickly at the quoted price.

The properties of these financial instruments differ dramatically from the physical assets mentioned above. Stock prices are quoted every day in the newspapers while the value of an art object is not known for sure unless it is sold. Before the sale, the best estimate an investor can get is from a professional appraisal or an opinion. Moreover, a common stock can be sold within minutes of the decision; a painting would be sold through auction or a gallery and it may take months, or even years, between the decision to sell and the day you get your money.

Real estate, antiques, and similar investments fall somewhere between paintings and securities in terms of know-

5

ing the value of the object at any time, and your ability to turn that estimate into cash.

Each of the three major categories of financial instruments has a place in every investment strategy. The reason is that each offers a different return and involves a different risk for the investor. To be certain that we are in agreement about what we mean by these instruments we will take a moment to describe them.

Short-term Instruments

U.S. Treasury Bills—obligations of the federal government that mature in 90 days or less—are the archetypical short-term instrument. Other short-term investments include bank obligations, called certificates of deposit; obligations of corporations, called commercial paper; and money market funds. These last are pools of money contributed by individual investors which are then used to purchase other short-term securities.

The important characteristic of short-term instruments is that they mature in a relatively short period of time—usually less than 90 days. As a result they are the safest of all investments. Remember that you will get back all of the money you invested plus the interest you earned in a short period of time, therefore, the price changes during the time that you own these instruments is not likely to be great.

The **yield** (also called the return or interest rate) offered by a short-term security put on the market today can be very different from what was offered yesterday or what will be offered tomorrow. The reason is that the demand for short-term credit by corporations, banks, or the U.S. Treasury and the available supply of money to meet these credit needs can change quickly. During 1982 (an extreme example it is true) short-term yields were as high as 18 percent and as low as 8 percent.

Treasury Bills differ from other short-term securities in that they sell at a discount from their face value. The interest you earn is the difference between the price you pay and the par or face value. For example, if a $1,000 Treasury Bill that matures in 90 days sells for $980, you will receive $1,000 or $20 more than you paid for it. If you did this four times a year you would earn $80 on your original $980 investment for an effective 8.89 percent interest.

Certificates of Deposit are a second popular short-term investment. These are issued by banks and (up to values of $100,000) are guaranteed by the federal government. Both the interest rate and the exact date of maturity are negotiated between the investor and the bank. As a result, a careful investor can plan to have the Certificate of Deposit fall due at exactly the date at which the funds are needed.

Money market funds are another popular and convenient short-term investment. When an investor buys into a money market fund he technically buys shares of the fund. The fund then uses the accumulated money to buy Certificates of Deposit, Treasury Bills, or other short-term instruments. Each day the fund earns some interest on its investments and, after deducting its operating expenses, the remainder is passed on to its investors in the form of a dividend.

Money market funds are very easy to use. They are similar to a bank checking account — you can write checks against your account, you can make regular deposits, and you automatically receive the daily interest on the amount you have in the account.

Bonds are offered by the federal, state, or local governments and by corporations. Obligations maturing in ninety days to two years are called short-term bonds; those maturing in two to five years are called intermediate-term bonds; and bonds maturing in more than five years are called long-term bonds.

Long-term Securities (Bonds)

The dollar amount of interest paid to the owner of a bond is fixed — say $100 per $1,000 of face value. However, the bonds themselves may be bought or sold and the price of a bond can fluctuate over a wide range. As a result the effective interest rate that is earned on a bond changes depending on the purchase price. Consider a $1,000 face-value bond that pays $100 per year and matures in five years. The seller of the bond commits himself to pay you $100 at the end of each year for a period of five years plus the $1,000 face value at the end of the fifth year. As the buyer of a bond you are a lender and you must decide how much you want to earn on the money you are lending. If 10 percent is a satisfactory return you would be willing to buy the bond for $1,000 since it will pay you $100 per year (10 percent) for five years. If you wanted your money to earn 15 percent you would offer less for the bond— $832.39 would be about right.

Let's see if this is correct. You can use one of the programs listed in the appendices but for this example we'll do it by hand. To duplicate the $100 interest payments you would have to invest $335.22 today at 15 percent (Table 2.1). To duplicate the $1,000 final payment of the face value would require an investment of $497.17 today at 15 percent interest (Table 2.2). The sum of $335.22 and $497.17 is $832.39. In other words, this is what the $1,000 face value bond paying $100 each year is worth *to you* if you want to earn a 15 percent return on your money.

Table 2.1. Invest $335.22 at 15 percent interest and take out $100 per year

End of Year	Reinvested Interest	Payment	Balance
0	0	0	$335.22
1	+50.28	−100	285.50
2	+42.83	−100	228.33
3	+34.25	−100	162.58
4	+24.39	−100	86.96
5	+13.04	−100	0.00

Table 2.2. Invest $497.17 at 15 percent interest to be worth $1000 in five years

End of Year	Reinvested Interest	Balance
0	0	$ 497.17
1	+ 74.58	571.75
2	+ 85.76	657.51
3	+ 98.63	756.14
4	+113.43	869.57
5	+130.43	1,000.00

To repeat, if you expect to earn 15 percent interest on your money you would only be willing to pay $832.39 for this bond; if you were willing to accept 10 percent interest you would pay $1,000; if you were willing to accept less than 10 percent you could pay more than $1,000.

The implications of this relationship are long-ranging and important. In a period when interest rates are rising, bond prices will fall sharply and an investor may experience heavy losses. When interest rates are falling, bond prices will rise, and an investor can make substantial profits. **Obviously it pays to own bonds when interest rates are falling and to switch to some other instrument when they are rising.**

Another important aspect of bond values is that the longer the time to maturity of a bond that pays a fixed sum each year, the greater is its price volatility when prevailing market interest rates change. You saw that for the five-year bond in Tables 2.1 and 2.2 the price would change from $1,000 to $832.39 if prevailing interest rates rose from 10 percent to 15 percent. If the same $1,000 bond were paying $100 per year for ten years, the current price would fall from $1,000 at 10 percent interest to $749.06 at 15 percent interest.

Thus, in periods of rising interest rates, wise investors will reduce the maturity periods of their portfolios — sell long-term bonds and buy short-term instruments such as a money market fund. In periods of falling interest rates the investor should move out of the money market fund and into long-term bonds.

Common Stocks

Stocks are shares in a corporation. They do not have a fixed lifetime but may be kept as long as the corporation remains in business. Stocks do not pay a fixed return each year; their dividends depend on the profitability of the corporation and the decisions of the management.

The price of a stock is based on your estimate of how much the stock will bring when you decide to sell it, how large the dividend stream will be while you hold it and, as we have seen earlier, the rate of return which you can earn if you invest in an alternative instrument. Since your feelings about these things may change radically over time, the price that you are willing to pay for a share of common stock can also vary widely.

Suppose you want to earn 15 percent return on a stock that now pays $2 per year in dividends. Further, suppose you expect the dividends to increase at the rate of 8 percent per year, and that in five years you believe you will be able to sell the stock for $30. Under these conditions, you would be willing to pay $21.62 for the stock today.

To see that this is the correct price, let's go through the same process that we did to calculate the price of a long-term bond.

Once again we divide the price that we would be willing to pay into two parts. The first is for the stream of payments that we will receive as long as we hold the instrument. The second is for the ending value that we will receive if we choose to sell it.

If the stock's $2 dividend grows at 8 percent per year and we want a 15 percent return, we would be willing to pay $7.70 for the dividend part of the return (Table 2.3). If the price in five years is $30 it is equivalent to $14.92 today (Table 2.4). The total—$7.70 for the dividends and $14.92 for the final value—is the current price of $21.62.

If you can buy it for less than this you will have found a bargain—you will earn more than 15 percent on your investment. If you pay more and the dividends and final value are as you anticipate, you will have earned less than 15 percent.

We have not discussed why you might expect the stock to be worth $30 five years from now, or why the dividends will continue to grow. We will get to these matters later. But the example highlights two important aspects of a successful stock-picking strategy. First, if the earnings

Table 2.3. Invest $7.70 at 15 percent interest and take out yearly dividends

End of Year	Reinvested Interest	Dividend	Balance
0	0.00	0.00	$7.70
1	+1.16	−2.00	6.86
2	+1.03	−2.16	5.72
3	+0.86	−2.33	4.25
4	+0.64	−2.52	2.37
5	+0.35	−2.72	0.00

Table 2.4. Invest $14.92 at 15 percent interest
to be worth $30 in five years

End of Year	Reinvested Interest	Balance
0	0	$14.92
1	+2.24	17.16
2	+2.57	19.73
3	+2.96	22.69
4	+3.40	26.09
5	+3.91	30.00

of a company are substantial, the company will be able to pay ever-larger dividends in succeeding years and so it is almost certain that you will be able to sell the stock at a higher price than what you paid for it. Second, the price you pay today is a critical factor in determining whether you will make a satisfactory return on your investment. Even if the company earns enough to pay increasing dividends, if you pay a very high price for the stock there may be no room for future price growth.

Some Conclusions

We can now examine the significant differences between short-term instruments, bonds, and stocks:

1. The price of a bond depends on three factors —the size of the interest coupon, the maturity date, and the return you want to receive. Two of these factors are known—the interest coupon and the maturity date. The third factor is yours to determine.

2. The price of a stock depends on four factors— the size of its current dividend, how the dividend will change in time, the price you expect to receive for the stock when you sell it, and the return you want to receive. Only one of these four factors is known—the current dividend. You must estimate how dividends will be paid in the future and what the future price of the stock will be.

It is easy to see why stocks are inherently more risky than bonds—there is much less known about their financial behavior. Stocks are also potentially more rewarding than bonds because the future values are not fixed but may increase in time.

Chapter 3

Investments and the Business Cycle

In managing your portfolio, how should you allocate your funds among Treasury bills, long-term bonds, and common stocks? The answer depends on your judgment about how interest rates will change, how the economy as a whole is moving, your need for current income, and your tolerance of risk.

It has been well established that the economy moves in cycles of recession and boom, usually three to five years in length. Short-term interest rates lag the business cycle by a few months. When the economy is climbing out of a recession, business firms restock their inventories, step up purchases of equipment and machinery, consumers buy cars or homes or large appliances and therefore increase their debt, and governments begin new building projects such as schools, parks, roads. All of this expansion involves an increase in loan activity; with the increased demand for funds there is a rise in interest rates (Figure 3.1).

As the recovery continues, short-term interest rates continue to rise but now a new factor enters the picture. Not only does demand for funds remain high but, as the economy expands, the Federal Reserve begins to restrict the supply of funds. It is attempting to curb price increases that are appearing in bottleneck sectors of the economy. The combination of high demand and tight supply of funds causes an even more rapid rise in interest rates.

Eventually, however, interest rates get so high that corporations won't accept them. This is because the business manager finds that he or she can't make enough profit with the borrowed funds to pay such high interest.

Figure 3.1.   Business activity is never so smooth and neat as drawn here, but many researchers have observed a cycle that repeats every three to five years on average. Interest rates reach their peaks some time after business activity peaks, and interest rates begin their climb only some time after business activity resumes.

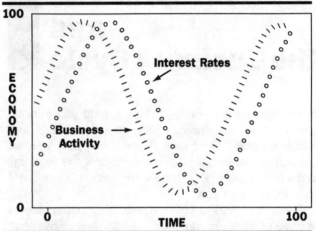

The economy now softens and growth slows, approaching a peak. Not all borrowing is affected at the same time: Federal, state, and local governments may have instituted long-term projects that need funds and consumers may continue to borrow. The Federal Reserve will almost certainly keep credit tight in an effort to curb inflation, so short-term interest rates continue to rise slowly, even after business activity starts to slow down.

Some time after the business cycle passes its peak — perhaps a few months, perhaps as much as a year — short-term interest rates turn down and may drop precipitously. At this point companies are cautious and reluctant to expand their debt until they are more sure they will be able to use the money profitably in new production equipment, for example, so demand continues to soften. The Federal Reserve attempts to encourage the recovery with an easier money policy. The combination of weak demand and an easier money supply keeps short-term interest rates low until well after the economy turns up.

This cycle provides clear guidelines as to how to manage an investment portfolio. We divide the cyclic

Figure 3.2. Distinctly different investment strategies are called for depending on the stage of the business cycle and the behavior of interest rates. Segment A calls for a predominance of short-term securities like Treasury Bills and money-market funds; in segment B the investor will have shifted to long-term bonds; segment C is when stocks are at their lowest and will be moving up in price.

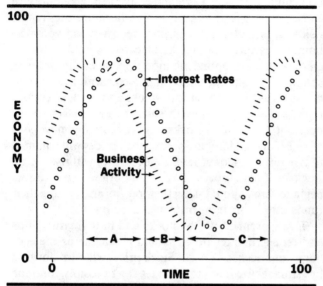

pattern into three segments. Segment A (Figure 3.2) is the peak of interest rates. During this period bond prices are lowest so as to keep their fixed interest payments competitive with the short-term interest rates. Common stock prices may begin to decline near the the peak of the business cycle because dividends as a percent of stock price are not growing as fast as they had been and in some sectors may even begin to fall. At this time your portfolio should be heavily weighted in favor of short-term instruments that are paying at peak levels. Not only will you earn a high current return on your funds but because the maturity of the portfolio is short you are liquid and will be in a position to take advantage of low-priced stocks or bonds when it is time to buy.

Segment B is when the economy goes into a real decline and interest rates follow. Now you should shift the emphasis into long-term bonds. Bond prices will rise off their low values and if you can catch them early enough you may be able to lock in a high return while short-term interest rates plummet.

Segment C is when the economy begins to give hints of bottoming out. Interest rates are still falling, bond prices will be high, stock prices are probably at or approaching their lows. Certain sectors of the economy give early indications of recovery—high fashion stores report rising sales and profits, airlines report rising volumes, home sales turn upward, plant capacity utilization increases. A more optimistic mood pervades the business community. Expectation of improved earnings and dividends turns investors back to stocks and stock prices rise rapidly. This is the time to shift the emphasis of your portfolio to common stocks. As the economy moves out of recession and into prosperity, stock prices will continue to rise but at a slower rate. Interest rates will rise. Some stocks will have moved to very high prices and investors begin to think about taking their profits and putting their funds into short-term instruments again.

This movement out of stocks and into Treasury Bills and money market funds should accelerate as the economy approaches its peak. Stock prices will turn down as investors realize that growth rates can't possibly continue at the rate they have been going.

Timing The general strategy for moving funds between the three basic instruments is:

1.   During peaks of the business cycle invest in Treasury Bills and money market funds.

2.   During the initial stages of economic turndown shift to long-term bonds.

3.   At the bottom of the recession and initial growth stages buy common stocks.

You may very properly ask, "How am I supposed to know when the economy is approaching its peak or when it has bottomed out and is about to turn up? Economists are notoriously bad forecasters—how am I expected to be wiser even than they?"

As a practical matter we hedge our bets. Hold some stock, some bonds, some short-term instruments at all times. What we are talking about here is only a shift in emphasis from period to period. Suppose your personal income and liquidity requirements are such that, on average, you want to hold 25 to 50 percent of your funds in short-term instruments. The above analysis suggests that at the peak of the business cycle this proportion could rise to 50 or 70 percent. Similarly, if you hold between half and two-thirds of your funds in common stock most of the time, you can consider raising the proportion to 75 percent or even 90 percent at the bottom of a recession. We'll be more specific about these proportions in later chapters.

There are, however, a number of indicators that provide hints as to where we are in the business cycle and the direction in which the economy is likely to move. These would include community sentiment, financial statistics, and economic activity.

Community Sentiment

When the economy is at or near a peak there is a general air of optimism which is evident everywhere. Friends will talk about how well they have done in real estate, the stock or commodities market, gold, paintings. Newspapers carry articles about a boy genius who, at the age of 26, made millions in a company started in his basement. There is a speculative mood that many people seem to share.

At the bottom of the business cycle your friends will talk about their losses in real estate, the stock or commodities market, gold, paintings. Newspapers write about the large firm or prominent person who is in serious financial difficulty. The atmosphere is gloomy and lawyers make jokes about how bankruptcy has become a growth industry.

There is also a curious perversity in the way the economy moves. Often positive community sentiment is at its peak just before a major downturn and at its most gloomy just before the recovery. The reasons stem from financial and economic causes.

Financial Statistics

Interest rates are a sure index to where the economy is and where it is going. At the peak of the cycle, short-term interest rates will be high and rising. They are higher than long-term rates even though the long-term rates themselves will be higher than they have been for some time. The reason is that the speculative fever leads to large borrowing for new ventures. One of the reasons the boom comes to an end is precisely because interest rates are so high they put an excessive burden on new projects.

At the bottom of the cycle we have exactly the reverse situation. Short term rates are low and lower than the long-term rates. Banks and other lenders are aggressively seeking credit-worthy borrowers. The combination of low interest rates and available money is one of the factors that leads to the turnaround. As firms borrow and expand, and consumers borrow and buy, the pace of economic activity quickens.

Economic Activity

The measures most often used to gauge the health of the economy are unemployment, industrial production, and gross national product. When the unemployment rate is low and falling, and industrial production and gross national product set new records for several successive quarters, the economy is judged to be moving briskly and maybe approaching a peak. When the unemployment rate is rising and industrial production and the gross national product decline for several quarters, we are heading toward recession.

We know a lot about our economy and its inherent instability, yet economists have not been able to do much about it. Each business cycle is marked by its own special characteristics and economists can, after the fact, document what these distinguishing features were. From an investor's point of view it is important to realize that the stock market tends to lead the parade — rising before the economy turns up, and falling before the economy turns down.

It is impossible to forecast consistently the month, or even the quarter, when the economy turns from one direction to another, but it is not necessary to be so accurate. You can protect your gains and minimize your losses by maintaining a well-distributed portfolio whose proportions in bonds, stocks, and money market instruments change in response to the larger sweeps of the economic cycles and not to every zig or zag of the charts.

Chapter 4

The Balanced Portfolio

Well-managed investment portfolios will have some combination of three objectives. A portfolio will be a source of cash to meet planned or unexpected demands; it will provide additional current income; it will preserve and enhance your wealth. The importance of each objective will depend on your age and other personal circumstances.

To achieve these objectives we have available to us three main categories of financial instruments—short-term instruments, long-term bonds, and common stocks. As we have seen, these instruments differ in their ability to achieve the objectives and in the way they act during different stages of the business cycle. We believe that *every* investor should have *some* percentage of his or her portfolio in all three categories. The proportion that is appropriate for you will be found in your answers to the following four questions:

1. How much liquidity—ready cash—do you need at all times?

2. Are there large demands for cash that you can foresee at some specified times in the future?

3. How much regular current income must the portfolio provide?

4. What is the current state of the business cycle? We will examine each of these considerations in turn.

Liquidity

The first concern for anyone managing a pool of money is to decide how much should be held in readily available form. You would place this amount in a safe, short-term, asset such as a money market fund, a Treasury Bill, or a Certificate of Deposit.

Faced with the 1982 recession many people realized they could easily lose their jobs. If all of their savings are tied up in their homes or in stocks they might well be forced to sell at a time when home and stock values were very low. If some portion of their savings had been held in short-term instruments it would be a lot easier to weather the storm.

Holding some portion of your savings in liquid assets doesn't mean that you forego the earning power of these funds. Money invested in a money market fund, Treasury Bill, or Certificate of Deposit earns interest that can be reinvested or used to supplement your regular income. The only disadvantage is that the interest so earned will vary from period to period and at certain stages of the business cycle may not be as high as you could earn in other ways. In the early 1970s, the yield on Treasury Bills was less than 5 percent. However, in 1981 and 1982 Treasury Bills paid over 14 percent and even at the end of 1982, when the rate fell, it was still over 10 percent.

Specific Cash Needs

If you know you will need a large sum to pay a school tuition bill or to repay a loan, a part of your portfolio can be segregated and invested in such a way as to meet this outlay when needed. Suppose your daughter will start college in two years and you will need $8,000 that September to pay the tuition bill. If current interest on Certificates of Deposit is 10 percent you could invest $6,611.57 today in one that matures just before the tuition is due and know that the $8,000 will be available when needed. (Note that $6,611.57 is the present value of $8,000 in two years at 10 percent interest.)

However, it is not advisable to manage a portfolio so conservatively if the need for funds is less precise or in the more distant future. We know a couple who are now in their early fifties and expect to retire in ten or 15 years and buy a house in the sunbelt. Should they invest all of their savings in a fifteen-year bond and plan to use the proceeds from the sale of the bond to buy their new home?

We think not. Certainly they should be making some provision for the future but they cannot be certain about how much they will need and they would be giving up flexibility by holding only a single bond for so long a period of time.

Income

Just how dependent are you on the portfolio for current income? If you have a good job you will be less interested in the income generated by the portfolio than in seeing the portfolio grow. On the other hand if you are a free-lance writer or a lawyer struggling to get a practice off the ground you may need some contribution from the portfolio to tide you over low-earning periods.

Stocks can be expected to provide larger returns in dividends and capital gains than long-term bonds or Treasury Bills. With due regard to the business cycle, stocks will take the larger share of the portfolio when growth is the primary objective. However, bonds offer the highest and most stable current return and are more appropriate for the free-lance writer or the struggling lawyer who needs to supplement an unreliable income.

The Business Cycle

In the last chapter we discussed how the three major categories of instruments perform during the various stages of the business cycle. We can give you a general sense of how a portfolio should be divided among the instruments for the average investor (Table 4.1).

Table 4.1. Portfolio proportions and the business cycle

Stage of the Business Cycle	Stocks	Short-term Instruments	Bonds
At the peak	10%	70%	20%
Heading down	25	25	50
At the bottom	75	5	20
Starting up	50	35	15
Approaching the peak	20	20	60

Individual needs will shift these proportions, particularly when there is a need for current income or for a specific amount at some time in the future. Note that with this plan the investor is never completely out of any of the instruments. The reason is that you cannot be certain how long a particular stage of the business cycle will last, or even exactly where you are in it. You hold the proportions to provide flexibility and to protect yourself against shifts.

Looking back at the performance of your portfolio you will always be able to figure out how you could have done better than you did. If business is at its peak why hold any stocks at all? If interest rates are rising, why hold any long-term bonds?

There is an old Wall Street expression, "He who looks backward dies of grief."

Investing is not a competitive sport. You are not trying to beat the Dow, or to make more money than the next person. It is to achieve reasonable financial objectives with a minimum of risk. That means some part of your portfolio will always be in the wrong instrument, but hopefully the smallest part.

Investment Discipline

 It is one thing to recognize that the proportions that you hold in various instruments should change over the business cycle, it is quite another to have the discipline to act on this knowledge.

Consider the problem of selling common stocks as the economy approaches a peak. If you held common stocks during the expansion stage of the cycle, you are likely to have many that have increased in value. As the economy continues to race toward the peak, your natural tendency will be to hold onto the stocks just a little longer. Rather than begin to sell off some of the stocks and shift your emphasis to short-term money market instruments, you will be inclined to think that since the stocks have gone up in the past and business conditions are so good, they will continue to rise.

Moreover, there are considerations other than the stages of the business cycle that are likely to influence your decision. Suppose you have short- term gains on many of your stocks. If you sell, the short-term gains will be taxed as ordinary income but if you wait a few more months until the short- term gains become long-term gains you will pay less in taxes. The risk of waiting a little longer is that the short-term gain may disappear as the economy turns.

Investing is a continuous struggle between fear and greed. We are afraid we may lose what we already have; we hope to be able to acquire just a little bit more. There is only one resolution to the dilemma and that is to develop an investment discipline. You must recognize that neither you nor anyone else is smart enough (or lucky enough) always to sell at the peak and buy at the bottom. That means you should act based on your best evaluation of the situation and then accept your errors philosophically. Decide on the proportions of your portfolio for each instrument at each stage of the business cycle (the ratios we recommend as a starting point are shown in Table 4.1). Use your best guess as to what stage the business cycle is at right now, and then shift your portfolio accordingly.

Stick to your guns. Stay with your own conclusions. The surest way to lose money is to constantly flip-flop between buying and selling. This is called "churning." It will make your broker rich and burn away your estate in a matter of a few years. Remember that you will make more money in the long run by trying to minimize your losses rather than trying to maximize your gains.

Chapter 5

Strategy and the Stages of Life

The investment strategy that is most appropriate for you depends primarily on your current income and age. To see how you would modify your strategy in response to these two factors we will follow an investment program for John Drew during the major stages of his life. John is a fiction but his life is similar to that of many successful Americans today.

During these years John was busy with urgent and important educational and career-starting problems. He graduated from school, bought a car, found a job, married. Planning an investment portfolio was the furthest thing from his mind. 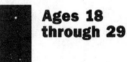 **Ages 18 through 29**

Shortly after he married, John was approached by a former classmate who persuaded him to buy a small life insurance policy. John wasn't really sure he needed the policy—his wife had a good job and if something happened to him she was quite capable of supporting herself. But John's friend pointed out that the policy could be converted at any time to one that remains in force if John were incapacitated by illness or accident—a situation that would otherwise make him uninsurable. For this reason, and to help his classmate, and to some extent because he felt it was part of growing up and making a family, John signed up for the policy.

Once a week John played doubles at a local tennis club and his usual partner was a stock broker. From time to time the stock broker told John about a low-priced stock that had the potential to appreciate in price because the company was doing some exciting new thing. One Sunday the stock broker caught John with a tax refund check hanging heavy in his bank account. John bought 100 shares of a computer software publisher at $4.50 a share. Six months later, he sold the stock for $8 a share, making a capital gain of $350 before commissions and personal income taxes.

His next experience was not so satisfactory. John took a flyer on 200 shares of a company in the oil and gas exploration business. He paid $6 a share and eighteen months later sold it for $4 a share.

Comments These two forays into the stock market cannot be considered anything approaching a planned investment strategy. From time to time John found himself with a little extra money. If he could make a substantial gain, that was wonderful. It could pay for a vacation to the Caribbean or a new stereo. If he lost it all, it would be no tragedy. He had a job and could replace the losses with future earnings.

At this stage of his life, John was more interested in a car or a house than he was in stocks, bonds, or insurance. If he experienced a small loss it would not affect his lifestyle. If he made a profit it would probably be spent at once on a desired luxury.

John's investment philosophy during these years can be classified as high risk/high reward. The amount of pleasure he could derive from making a little money far exceeded the pain he would experience if he lost. His thinking went something like, "I can double or triple my investment if things work out according to plan. The most I can lose is a few dollars and most likely I'll break even."

But he was wrong. When he made a profit he would rarely make as much as he hoped, and when he lost he would probably lose a lot more than he expected. However, if the sums involved were small, the impact — positive or negative — would be minor.

Sometime during this career- and family-establishing period John can be expected to reflect on what he has been doing about building a nest egg. This will lead to a somewhat more sophisticated approach to his personal finances.

At the age of 33 John was promoted and was considered by colleagues and supervisors to have a real future with the company. He had more responsibility and power in his new job and he began to bring in more money.

When his first child was born John bought a condominium and two years later, when the second child came along, he sold the condominium and bought a house. He also increased his insurance coverage to provide more financial security for his family.

John continued to do business with his stock broker friend. Early in the period he bought a couple of long-term corporate bonds because interest rates were high. At 35 he purchased his first municipal bond since the interest payments were exempt from federal taxes — an increasingly important factor as his income levels moved him up through the tax rate structure. He also bought common stocks from time to time and made money on some and lost on others.

By the time he reached his late thirties John was seriously dissatisfied with his stock broker and then with himself as an investor. He began to think about accumulating wealth for his children's education and for his own purposes. Specifically, he wanted to increase the range of his options — to cover himself if there was a serious illness in the family, to buy a vacation home, to quit his job and invest in his own business if the right situation presented itself. Suddenly the opportunity uses of real capital were all around him and he felt severely limited by his lack of funds.

In his early forties, therefore, John decided to formulate an investment plan and he came up with a simple and satisfactory one — from that point on, he decided, he would only buy municipal bonds for the tax-free income, and common stocks of companies that he considered "emerging growth" companies. These are smaller, less well established companies that take the bulk of their resources and revenues from industries with high growth potential. Whether or not the companies paid a dividend was of less importance than the fact that they would continue, or move into, a period of high profitability.

Comments From our point of view the most significant development during this period is that John Drew was motivated by his achievements and ambitions toward a new level of financial sophistication and maturity. He faced some basic truths one of which was that his broker frequently gave him bad advice. It wasn't that his broker deliberately misled him; rather, his friend was so enthusiastic about a company and told so glowing a story that John bought the stock without much attention to the price he was paying for it. John found himself whipsawed by the articles he read in business magazines. The reporters always seemed to be able to find something exciting about the companies they discussed, and either said outright or at the least implied that these were companies whose stock prices would surely rise. More often than not, the predictions were not fulfilled, but by that time the reporters were writing about some new company with even brighter prospects. John came to realize that most of these hot tips resulted in losses rather than gains.

John soon discovered that because of his own increasing financial sophistication in his job he could gauge the health of a company more accurately than his broker could. His friend still talked about "hot new issues," about "high-tech" industries, about rumored mergers and tender offers. John could now read a balance sheet or operating statement with more patience for the footnotes and a healthy skepticism about special items.

John also realized that once he bought a stock or bond, he didn't know when to sell it. Should he take a current profit or wait? Should he sell when the price went down or wait until it returned to what he paid for it? While his broker was very free with advice on buying, he was much less free with suggestions about selling.

John could be very analytical in most other buy/sell decisions — when to sell his house, when to sell his car. He knew when he should make a commitment of time and resources to a potential business prospect and when to move on. Why could he not be as clear about his investments?

Over the years John learned several things from his investment experience. First, stock prices seldom moved up as much as the broker thought they would, and frequently they fell sharply and unexpectedly. Second, the stocks that paid regular dividends seemed far more stable in price than those that did not, and the dividend checks were pleasant to receive so reliably. While he had to pay taxes on this income, one year he was able to take a vacation with a dividend from a small appliance manufacturer, and put a down payment on a new car with the dividend paid by a camera company.

Finally, he came to recognize that he would have to take responsibility for his own investment decisions. He and his family would reap the rewards from the correct ones and take the lumps from the wrong ones. Under these circumstances he decided he needed a plan that would set his objectives, establish an acceptable level of risk, and target a desired level of income from his investments.

He was no longer interested in a quick killing but was still determined to take aggressive business risks. He wanted to build his capital but do so prudently. Current income from the portfolio would take second place to the hope that his estate would be substantial in a reasonable number of years.

In middle and late middle age John Drew and his wife came to terms with themselves and their own limitations. John realized that he would never be the head of the company for which he worked, though he would continue to have an important role to play in its future. He could not expect ever to be wealthy but he was assured of a comfortable income as long as he wished to stay on the job.

Ages 45 through 59

John's entire financial philosophy shifted radically in a few short years. He had reached his peak earning power and with his wife's salary the combined family income was very substantial. They were both less concerned about their own financial future than they were about their children's—jobs, family, happiness.

By his late fifties John was more interested in protecting what he had accumulated than in adding still more. The mortgage was nearly paid off; his insurance policies were more than adequate to provide for his wife and family; he had a vacation home; he was a member of a golf club;

he was active in local civic organizations. He liked his lifestyle and wanted to keep it.

The investment strategy appropriate to this period is less concerned with building wealth and more with minimizing losses to inflation or economic downturns. He increased his holdings of municipal bonds and changed his stock portfolio from emerging growth companies to quality growth companies. These are the largest, best managed companies in each industry. John thought that if he bought these companies he could stop worrying about when and if they should be sold. Investing in good, solid companies meant his risk exposure would be minimal.

Comments The transformation from a growth-oriented strategy to a preservation strategy meant that the business risk that had previously been acceptable was no longer so. The joy from taking capital gains was more than offset by the pain resulting from capital losses.

John made two major policy changes in his portfolio. First, he increased the percentage of municipal bonds — with the family income at a peak, every additional dollar had to be protected from the very high tax rates. Second, he hoped the concentration on quality growth companies would reduce potential losses. If he bought these companies with care and avoided paying too high a price for them, he should be able to conserve his wealth.

In short, John adopted a conservative investment strategy. However, since he never developed a good understanding of when to sell a stock, he may still have assumed more risk than he thought. Even the largest companies experience some fluctuation in price. As we have seen in several instances recently, large and highly respected companies may come upon hard times or their managements may make bad decisions. Sears, IBM, Texas Instruments, Phillips Petroleum, International Harvester, all experienced substantial price declines, at least temporarily, in recent years.

Ages 60 through 70 As John and his wife approached and entered retirement their portfolio changed again. Their children were starting families of their own and John and his wife considered how they would distribute their wealth. Should they leave it to the children or skip a generation and provide for the grandchildren? Were there charities or schools to which they had strong emotional attachments that they wanted to support? How much should they keep for their own needs? And what if their health began to fail?

Retirement meant a substantial drop in income. He became dependent on his pension plan, Social Security payments, and the investment portfolio. At these lower levels of income, tax-free investments were less attractive, so John sold some of his municipal bonds and increased his holdings in higher-yielding corporate bonds. In addition, John wanted to be more liquid so that he could meet unexpected demands from the children or his own or his wife's needs. He bought short-term government securities and reduced the proportion of stock in his portfolio. In short, he set up a highly liquid portfolio so that his estate was in order and he would always have enough ready cash to meet any contingency.

Comments

The shift from municipal bonds to Treasury Bills or short-term Certificates of Deposit increased liquidity while the shift to corporate bonds maximized current income. The kinds of stocks that remain in the portfolio need not be different than what he had been holding previously. If anything he could shift the emphasis even further toward dividend income as distinct from long-term growth.

Summary

An investment portfolio is not a static thing. It should change with income, age, and other circumstances. Your attitude toward risk will also change and the portfolio must respond accordingly. What we will be doing in this book is to provide guidance in the determination of the best strategy and show how it may be successfully and safely executed.

1. We will help you examine the factors in your life now and in the immediate future that establish the acceptable level of risk. What kind of return is important to you at this time—current income, capital growth, or tax-free income?

2. Different financial instruments provide different patterns of return now and in the future. What are these

patterns and which will best meet your objectives?

3.   How should the proportion of stocks, bonds, and short-term financial instruments in your portfolio change in time and in relation to the business cycle and how do you monitor these proportions?

4.   What investment strategy for common stocks should you follow—capital gains or current income, or are they equally important?

5.   How do you actually execute a strategy? What tools are available for classifying stocks and monitoring their performance?

Chapter 6

Case I
A Young Couple

Your portfolio generally should have all three — short-term money market instruments, bonds, and common stocks. The percentage allocated to each instrument depends on the stage of the business cycle and on your individual circumstances.

Short-term instruments should dominate during the peak of the business cycle; this is when interest rates are highest. When the economy is heading toward recession, interest rates will fall and you can shift out of short-term instruments and into long-term bonds. As the recession approaches bottom and goes into a climb, the portfolio should be shifting toward stocks.

These are the underlying patterns we will use to allocate funds among the various instruments available. Specific financial needs will fine-tune the exact proportions placed in each instrument. For example, if your income varies from month to month you may want to hold a higher percentage of your portfolio in liquid assets. If you know that in two years you will have to make a large payment you can prepare for it now by buying a bond that matures just before the payment is due.

In this and the next five chapters, we will show how the patterns are adjusted to meet the needs of six personal situations. Obviously your situation will be different, but by following the steps outlined here you will be able to apply the principles to consistently maximize your earnings.

We develop a portfolio recommendation by answering four questions:

1. How much current income must the portfolio generate?

2. How much liquidity must be maintained at all times?

3. Are there any large cash demands that will be made on the portfolio at some specified date in the future?

4. What is the current stage of the business cycle?

David Alpern graduated from Purdue as a mechanical engineer six years ago. Upon graduation he landed a job with Finney & Abelson, Inc., a large contractor in the petroleum industry, and he now has a responsible position in the middle management of the company. David is well regarded by his supervisors; he has been through the management training program the company maintains for coming executives and is obviously earmarked for advancement. He currently earns $38,000 a year.

Susan graduated from Mount Holyoke four years ago and went to work for F&A's information systems department. It was there that she and David met and, after a short courtship, married. Susan earns $26,000 a year.

When he first took the job with F&A, David bought a condominium a short drive from the office. He paid $43,000 for it and estimates that it is now worth $55,000 though there is almost $35,000 remaining on the mortgage. The Alperns live in the condominum. They have no children but plan to start a family soon.

While the parents of both David and Susan are of moderate means, Susan has one grandfather who did well for himself. He owned a small machine tool shop and when he approached retirement he was able to sell the business to his largest customer, a local manufacturer. At the time of the sale Susan's grandfather made a will that provided $50,000 for each grandchild. A few months ago Susan's grandfather died and Susan expects to receive her inheritance shortly.

Current Income Requirements

The Alperns do not have a current income problem. Both earn good salaries and David is likely to continue to receive raises in the foreseeable future. If Susan left her job to give birth to a child and decided to stay at home for a few months or even a few years, they would still probably not have current income problems.

The inheritance may induce them to start the family earlier than originally planned, which means not only the medical expenses will have to be paid for over and above what their insurance covers, but also their lifestyle could change dramatically. They may decide to move to a larger home, they may need a second car, and Susan's earning power will be interrupted, at least temporarily. We would recommend that the Alperns set aside $20,000 of the inheritance — about the equivalent of nine months of Susan's salary — and put it in a money market fund or money-market bank account.

Liquidity Requirements

The Alperns have no foreseeable large expenses other than those associated with starting a family and we have covered that contingency with the $20,000 in the money market fund.

Future Lump Sum Requirements

The remaining $30,000 will be invested depending on the stage of the business cycle. We put only a small percentage in long-term bonds for the Alperns because they want their portfolio to both earn a return and to appreciate in value. Bonds would only be advisable during the downturn of a business cycle when stock prices are likely to be falling.

Stage of the Business Cycle

The Alperns are young and have every prospect of continuing to be high earners. Once their liquidity needs are provided for (by setting aside the $20,000), they should not seek additional current income so much as to increase the overall value of the portfolio.

Table 6.1.   Portfolio allocation for a young couple

Stage of Business Cycle	Stocks	Money Market	Bonds
At the peak	15%	75%	10%
Heading down	40	35	25
At the bottom	95	5	0
Starting up	80	20	0
Approaching the peak	25	70	5

These proportions differ from those of the "average" investor presented in Chapter 4 in several important ways:

1. The Alperns are advised to hold a larger percentage of equity than the average investor because they are young and can look toward a future of substantial opportunity. They can afford to take more risk than most. At the bottom of the business cycle, when the economy is in the doldrums, we recommend that they invest 95 percent of their funds in stocks, and even as the economy begins to recover we consider it wise to hold 80 percent of their portfolio in stocks.

2. The Alperns should use the money market as a temporary holding place for their funds. When buying opportunities appear in stocks, as when the economy begins to soften, they can draw on these liquid balances. As the economy approaches the peak they should be taking their profits, selling out, and storing their gains in the money market.

3. Long-term bonds will play a minor role in the Alpern's portfolio for these years. They have no need for the income that bonds provide and are more interested in overall portfolio growth. At the high end of the business cycle, when interest rates are at their peaks, they may choose to make a modest commitment to long-term bonds. As interest rates fall, however, they should sell the bonds and get back into stocks.

Other Young Investors

 The strategy recommended for young investors therefore takes into account their special circumstances. When you are young you can look forward to many years of substantial, and increasing, earnings. Further, current income is probably not a pressing problem and so you can afford to exchange the certainty of bond income for the potentially larger capital gains of the stock market.

It is important to stress that this is a risky strategy and not appropriate for everyone, or even for every young investor. It is designed to take maximum advantage of the cyclical moves in the economy and should be pursued only with funds that are not depended on for daily needs or for things like children's schooling.

Chapter 7

Case II
A Professional
Couple

Jim Clark, 59, is an upper level business executive. His salary, as vice president of a medium sized manufacturing company, is $65,000 a year. His wife, Mary, is a partner in a small law firm and her income is over $37,000 a year. Both Jim and Mary contribute to pension plans at their respective companies and when they retire they expect to receive roughly 40 percent of their terminal salaries in pensions.

The Clarks have two children, both grown. The eldest, Elizabeth, is married and starting her own family. The son, Paul, 23, was an unenthusiastic student who left college in his sophomore year to tour Europe. He returned to the U.S. late last year, and worked briefly as a part-time logger in Idaho. For three months now he has been a claims adjustor for an insurance company in Boise and he seems to enjoy both the job and the steady paycheck. The Clarks have not had to provide any financial assistance to Paul since he returned from Europe. However, Jim does support his widowed mother who is 78. She is an energetic and capable woman who lives alone in a rented apartment in Arizona.

The Clark's have accumulated $350,000 from an inheritance and savings. They own their home which has only a small mortgage remaining. How should they allocate the $350,000 among short-term instruments, bonds, and stocks?

The Clark's salaries total more than $100,000 a year and since both are in good health, they can expect to continue to earn at this level or higher until they retire. They need take no extraordinary

**Current
Income
Requirements**

risks to generate additional income from their portfolio. Indeed with their salary income so high they are probably looking for ways to hold taxes down on the income that may be generated from investments.

Liquidity Requirements

There are two reasons why the Clarks may want to hold a reasonable percentage of their assets in liquid funds. First, Jim's mother could suddenly make fairly heavy demands on their resources. Right now she is quite capable of caring for herself, but at 78 sickness or accident could quickly raise hospital bills and nursing care.

Second, Paul may have financial needs that his parents would want to help with. He is working and more or less financially independent, but if he should decide to go back to school or start his own business, the Clarks may want to be able to finance the venture.

To be prepared for these contingencies the Clarks should probably keep $25,000 to $30,000 in liquid assets. This represents one-quarter to one-third of their annual income and less than ten percent of their portfolio.

Future Lump Sum Requirements

From the information we have there is no reason to think they will have any other large demands for cash in the future. They may decide to buy another home or a condominium to use for retirement but presumably the sale of their present home would provide the necessary capital. More likely, the Clarks want to build and preserve their savings so as to protect their standard of living in the event of sickness or the loss of a job and for retirement. It is also likely that they are beginning to think about making some provision for the education of their grandchildren.

Stage of the Business Cycle

The Clarks' age and financial position suggest that considerations other than the business cycle will be more important in establishing the structure of their portfolio. The Clarks are well off and they want to stay that way; capital growth is much less important than safety.

Table 7.1. Portfolio allocation
for an older professional couple

Stage of Business Cycle	Stocks	Money Market	Bonds
At the peak	10%	50%	40%
Heading down	20	45	35
At the bottom	40	30	30
Starting up	30	40	30
Approaching the peak	20	45	35

Notice how different these proportions are from those recommended for the average investor (in Table 4.1) and for the young couple early in their careers (Table 6.1).

1. Unlike the average investor, the Clarks should hold a high percentage of their assets in short-term money market funds at all stages of the business cycle. This provides both safety and liquidity.

2. They should also hold a higher percentage in long-term bonds because the risk associated with these instruments is low. Tax-free municipal bonds will be more suitable than corporate bonds because the Clarks are in a high tax bracket. At the 50 percent tax rate a 7 percent interest rate from the municipal bond is equivalent to 14 percent in a taxable corporate bond.

3. The percentage of their portfolio held in equities is relatively modest at all stages of the business cycle but the pattern will shift in the same way, that is, it should be at a maximum when the economy is at the bottom and at a minimum when it approaches the top.

Older Professional Investors

Long-term bonds make up roughly a third of this portfolio at all times and as we have said, these should be tax-free municipals. By long-term bonds we mean bonds that will mature in 5 to 10 years. Short-term Treasury Bills should be between 30 and 50 percent of this portfolio at all times. This provides a hedge against changes in prevailing interest rates and a desirable liquidity.

To reduce risk, equities will take a smaller percentage of the portfolio—but smaller only in the context of what we recommended for the average investor. They will still want to take advantage of opportunities presented by changes in the business cycle. Note that at the bottom of the business cycle we recommend that 40 percent of their portfolio be invested in stocks.

Chapter 8

Case III
A Single Woman

Maria Gomez, 34, was the first of her family to graduate from college and then go on to law school. Her parents worked hard to help finance her education, and with the help of summer jobs and the fact that she was able to live at home while attending school, Maria completed her education without incurring any debt.

In her senior undergraduate year Maria married, but the marriage wasn't successful and after two difficult years she initiated divorce proceedings. Since they were childless, young, and without any assets to speak of, the divorce was quick and left no obligations either way.

It is now ten years since the divorce and Maria works in a small law firm making $38,000 a year. She specializes in personal injury work. She has developed a reputation as a solid and competent attorney and she expects to be promoted to junior partner.

Her personal future is less certain. She lives alone in a rented one-bedroom apartment. Somehow it seems smaller than it had when she first moved in and she is thinking about moving to a larger apartment in the same neighborhood. Her three-year-old car still runs well but it has begun to burn oil and she is concerned that repair bills may start coming in now that it has passed the 30,000 mile mark.

Maria has several close friends, male as well as female, and thinks vaguely that she will marry again someday, but at the moment she is still uninterested in so serious a commitment.

She does not have expensive tastes and her income is more than adequate for her needs. She can take vacations when and where she wants, takes herself and a friend to the theatre and or ballet now and then, and can eat out whenever she is so inclined.

Maria has been saving between $5,000 and $7,000 a year from her present salary, and has accumulated just over $30,000 since the divorce. She keeps the money in a money market fund because it never seemed enough to consider as a "portfolio," but during the past few weeks she has begun to ask friends about what they do with their savings.

One woman friend said she had bought a condominum and suggested that since Maria was thinking about moving anyway, that might be a good idea for her as well. But Maria didn't want to move to a different neighborhood or to the suburbs. A number of young professionals lived nearby and her family lived only a ten-minute drive away. She also didn't want to get involved with heavy mortgage payments and the problems of dealing with fellow condominium owners. The friend talked about capital gain when she sold the condominium but that didn't seem important to Maria at the moment.

A second friend said he had begun to invest in long-term municipal bonds because of their tax exempt status. Maria disliked paying taxes as much as anyone but she was also concerned about locking up her money for long periods of time with inflation eating away at it all the time.

A third friend liked the stock market. She had purchased a few shares of DuPont and General Motors several years back and had seen the stocks move up nicely in value. She now had her eye on several other stocks she was convinced would do equally well and when their prices dropped just a little she was planning to buy some shares in several. She offered to introduce Maria to her broker who always had a lot of ideas about what to buy or sell.

What should Maria do with her $30,000 and what plans should she make for her current savings program?

Current Income Requirements Maria's current salary and prospects were such that she was confident they would cover any immediate needs. She did not need to look for her investments to provide additional income.

Similarly, Maria saw no need to concern herself about future lump sum payments. Her parents were in good health and had enough money to take care of their needs. She might want to buy a new car fairly soon, but she could make the purchase at a convenient time—perhaps just after she gets her Christmas bonus.

Future Lump Sum Payments

Maria's greatest need is probably to preserve flexibility so that she can do what she wants to do when she wants to do it. If she were to marry she may want to help buy a house. While she likes her job, if the junior partnership doesn't come through soon, she might consider going into practice for herself and that would require start-up capital.

Liquidity Requirements

To preserve and enhance flexibility, Maria should consider investing in short-term to intermediate bonds and build a "ladder" of maturities. By this we mean that if she were to invest $20,000 in municipal bonds she should consider buying $5,000 worth that will mature in one year, another $5,000 that matures in two years, and so on. Then, one year from now, when the first bond matures she would buy a bond that matures in four years. By building such a ladder of maturities, she will have a bond at least once every year. Moreover, if her money is spread over four or five year maturities, she will be free of some of the risk associated with major swings in interest rates. She will always be earning the average short to intermediate rate rather than being dependent on the yield available from a bond bought at a single time.

Maria thinks she should put some money into stocks which will increase in value over time. However, it would be inefficient to invest $500 or $1,000 in ten or twenty different stocks. The transaction charges would take too large a percentage of each purchase or sale. On the other hand, if she were to invest larger sums in fewer stocks she would be speculating, not investing. Fortunately there is a ready solution available. It is to invest in a mutual fund which effectively puts her contributions into a well-diversified portfolio of individual stocks.

A mutual fund is one in which a number of investors pool their money to buy stocks. The funds are managed by professional fund managers. Each fund describes its objective in a prospectus and then proceeds to buy securities that are consistent with the stated objective. The value of the fund is calculated each day and the price is quoted in the newspapers. The shares that the investor owns can be sold back to the fund at any time at the quoted price. Mutual funds are therefore highly liquid assets.

If Maria buys bonds rather than stocks she will incur less risk at the cost of somewhat lower return. If she buys a mutual fund her risk is higher, but so is the potential return.

Maria must allocate her savings in accordance with her feelings about risk. If she is really concerned about losing her savings she would be well advised to put more of her money in the laddered maturity bonds. If she is willing to assume risk the mutual fund is a better direction.

As a single woman with no back-up other than her own savings and earning power, we would recommend that she put the bulk of her savings, say two-thirds, in the laddered maturity bond portfolio. The remaining third should be put into a mutual fund. Her monthly savings can go into a money market fund until it accumulates $5,000 or $10,000. Approximately once a year she can buy another bond or add the savings to her mutual fund account.

The reason we recommend the high proportion in bonds is that Maria needs the safety and independence that can only come from an investment that does not fluctuate sharply in value. She has already established a pattern of independence through education, divorce, and job. To maintain this independence she needs financial security. Once a good-sized bond portfolio has been established she will be able to live with a higher level of risk and increase the percentage of savings in stocks.

Stage of the Business Cycle

The changing phases of the business cycle need effect only a portion of Maria's portfolio.

The heavy percentage in bonds provides the needed safety, independence, and flexibility. The smaller percentage in equities offers growth. The minor

Table 6.1. Portfolio allocation for a single woman

Stage of Business Cycle	Stocks	Money Market	Bonds
At the peak	5%	25%	70%
Heading down	20	10	70
At the bottom	25	5	70
Starting up	20	10	70
Approaching the peak	10	20	70

changes with changes in the business cycle follow our recommendations for protecting the value of the higher risk portion of the portfolio.

As the total value of portfolio grows in time, Maria may want to increase the percentage held in stocks. Similarly if her personal circumstances change—if she marries, hangs out her shingle, chooses to buy rather than rent her home, the portfolio strategy may come to be more like one of the other situations we are describing in these cases.

Chapter 9

Case IV
A Single Parent

Jean Glover, 38, has custody of her two children, Stephen, 13, and Sandra, 11. Her former husband, from whom she has been divorced for two years, owns and operates a plastics extrusion plant. During the early years of their marriage Jean worked in the office with her husband and helped build the business. After the children were born Jean stayed at home. The business continued to prosper and at the time of the divorce was doing over $7 million in sales.

The divorce proceeding was long and bitter, but in the end Jean received title to the house and $200,000 in cash. In addition, she was awarded $2,000 a month from her husband for child support. On the advice of a friend, Jean put all the money in bank Certificates of Deposit and concentrated on rebuilding her life. She took courses at a community college nearby in preparation for returning to the business world.

In the meantime her former husband tried to expand into consumer products, however, because of inadequate capital and high interest rates his business suffered and he has begun to miss child support payments.

Jean would like to maintain the same standard of living she and her children previously enjoyed. She estimates that she needs $30,000 a year in pretax income to do so. When her former husband  **Current Income Requirements** became delinquent in his child support payments she retained a lawyer to keep after him, but despite the lawyer's efforts, she gradually came to realize that she would not receive all of the $24,000 each year stipulated in the divorce settlement — at least while his business was doing poorly. She had to look elsewhere for additional income and she wondered whether it could come from her $200,000 portfolio.

When Jean first put her money in bank Certificates of Deposit they were paying over 11 percent interest, so she received almost $23,000 a year in income. Since that time interest rates fell and their yield at the time of this analysis was only 8.5 percent. High quality long-term corporate bonds paid a little more — 10.5 percent, and dividends from common stocks were averaging about 5.5 percent. Therefore, if Jean put all of the $200,000 into long-term bonds she would earn $21,000; if she remained invested in bank Certificates of Deposit she would earn $17,000; and if she put the money in common stocks she might expect to receive $11,000 in dividends. Obviously Jean faces a serious income problem: no matter what the investment scheme, her $200,000 can't generate enough income to satisfy her needs. What is she to do?

Liquidity Requirements

Jean should be reluctant to put all of her money in long-term bonds even though they offer the largest current income. She must hold some part of her portfolio in more liquid instruments. She does not have a job producing a regular income and so she will be dependent on her portfolio and on the undependable child support payments from her former husband for the family's living expenses. Income from these sources does not arrive in regular installments, however, and the costs of food, clothing, telephone, heat electricity, house mortgage, must be paid monthly if not weekly.

It is our recommendation that Jean maintain a money market account large enough to cover living expenses for at least three months and preferably more. Since she expects her costs to be about $2,500 a month, she should keep between $7,500 and $10,000 in such an instrument at all times.

Future Lump Sum Requirements

One large expense on the horizon is the cost of the children's education. While the divorce agreement specifies that the husband is to bear these expenses, Jean wants to set up a contingency fund that will provide the money when it will be needed.

Tuition and school living costs are likely to rise and the total could be a substantial sum by the time her two children reach college age. Jean didn't think either child would qualify for scholarships, but they could be eligible for student loans if those were available at the time. If they worked part time during their college years they might be expected to get along with relatively little help from her. She did, however, want to be able to provide at least some assistance and this meant investing a part of the portfolio on the children's behalf. The more this investment appreciated in value, the larger the contribution could be made toward their school expenses.

Jean Glover faces difficult financial decisions. As we have seen, at the present time her portfolio cannot generate enough income to take care of her present needs, much less deal with the liquidity requirements and the children's college education. Either Jean must increase her income or cut back on her expenditures.

Stage of the Business Cycle

She could take a job and she plans to do this, but would prefer to finish her course work at the community college since that would make her eligible for a better, and possibly a higher-paying, job.

She could sell her home and invest the proceeds. Whether this is a wise course depends on how much she could get for the home and how much alternative housing would cost.

She could lower her expenditures and her standard of living, but before doing that she wanted to explore all other alternatives. She felt she was not a wasteful spender and, at least for the children's adolescent years, was resolved to do everything possible to stay in their home and maintain their current standard of living.

Critical in our recommendations for Jean Glover is the fact that her present plight is not permanent. Within a relatively short time she will be getting a job and begin to earn additional income. The children will be leaving home in a few years and this will not only reduce immediate expenses but make it possible for her to sell her home and move into smaller quarters. Moreover, her former husband's business might well improve and he may then resume the child-support payments at any time and take on the burden of their college educations. All of these possibilities suggest that she could meet at least a part of her current income needs by spending some of her capital.

Obviously spending capital to boost income is not a viable long-term strategy. It is only recommended when we can predict with some assurance that future income will be higher and future expenses lower. If she chooses this course, Jean must be careful to protect herself against large losses. Specifically, she should not place all her funds in long-term bonds even though they would provide a larger current return. Inflation would then hurt her in two ways. First, interest rates would rise and the market value of the portfolio would decline. Second, inflation would reduce the purchase power of her fixed income.

Similarly, she should not put all of her money in the stock market. She could do very well if the market were to rise; however, if she were wrong either in her timing or in her selections, she could lose an important part of her limited capital—something she cannot afford to do.

Thus, we would recommend that she put the bulk of her portfolio in short-term money market instruments. Though they do not currently yield enough to meet her expenses, they will provide the best compromise of income, liquidity, and security.

Table 6.1. Portfolio allocation for a single parent

Stage of Business Cycle	Stocks	Money Market	Bonds
At the peak	0%	50%	50%
Heading down	0	75	25
At the bottom	10	90	0
Starting up	15	85	0
Approaching the peak	5	70	25

Suppose the economy were approaching the peak of the market. Jean might put $10,000 in stocks, $40,000 in bonds, and $150,000 in the money market. She would earn $550 in dividends from the stocks and $4,200 from the bonds for a total of $4,750. She would take $2,100 from the money market fund so that at the end of the year she would have approximately $137,500 left after the average interest earned of approximately $1,000 per month.

At the end of the first year (assuming the economy is now at a peak) she would sell her stocks for $11,000 (assuming a 10 percent capital gains). Her portfolio is then $40,000 in bonds, $11,000 in cash, and $137,500 in the money market. She now increases her holdings in bonds to $95,000, leaving $94,000 in the money market account. Assuming interest rates haven't changed, during the second year she will have earned $10,000 from the bonds and taken $1,667 a month from the money market. Approximately $667 of the $1,667 would be supplied by interest on the balance so that at the end of the second year she would have approximately $82,000 left in the money market.

Her total portfolio value after two years has been reduced from $200,000 to $177,000. By this time she will have completed her courses and be able to take a job. If she can earn $15,000 or more at the job she will not need to draw down any further on her capital since the remaining $177,100 will earn $15,000 even at 8.5 percent, and proportionately more if interest rates have risen during this period.

Notice how different these recommendations are from those for the young couple or for the professional couple. To review the reasons:

1.   Jean Glover should maintain the larger percentage of her portfolio in short-term money market instruments during all stages of the business cycle. The additional income that might be produced by putting a larger share in long-term bonds is small but the additional risk would be very large. If she locked herself into a fixed return at the bottom of the cycle she would pay dearly in terms of lost opportunity when the economy recovered.

2.   She can invest a small percentage of her portfolio in common stocks to provide for her children's education, however, it is important that these investments be made at the proper time. If she invested when the economy was at or near the peak she would expose herself to substantial risk.

3. When she has finished her schooling and gets a job she can change her strategy to be more in line with that of the average investor. She would then take a somewhat longer view and begin to think about increasing her total portfolio value by making a larger commitment to stocks.

Case V
A Widow

Alice Johnson is 62 years old. For more than thirty years she worked side by side with her husband in their small office supply business. While they had many bad times over the years, on the whole the business provided them enough income to live comfortably and to put two sons through college—one is now an architect and the other a dentist. When Asa Johnson died, Alice was left owning the business but little else, since they had always thought of their business as their savings account and plowed back every penny they could into inventory or modernized facilities.

Her husband's death was unexpected, and Alice took a long time to recover from the shock. She was no longer interested in the business—or much of anything else for that matter—and so, with her disinterested permission, the boys sold the business to a competitor for $250,000.

After almost a year of mourning Alice finally began to recover, to look around and decide what she was going to do with the rest of her life. In addition to the $250,000, Alice's assets consisted of her home (the mortgage had long since been fully paid out) and social security payments. How should she invest the $250,000?

Alice saw no reason to move from her home. While large for one person, it was not so big as to be difficult to take care of, and she had many friends and relatives in the neighborhood which she did not want to leave.

**Current
Income
Requirements**

Her housing costs would therefore be limited to taxes and upkeep—heating, utilities, lawn care, insurance, and repair. Her other living expenses would be for food, clothing, transportation, medical care, income taxes, charities, and the gifts she liked to give to her grandchildren. Social Security payments made a substantial contribution to these expenses but Alice calculated she would need an additional $22,000 a year to live comfortably and she hoped her portfolio could generate at least this amount.

Liquidity

A second important consideration was that the portfolio be invested in as safe and as liquid a way as possible. She had several reasons for this: She was reaching an age when she might fall ill and have heavy medical bills that Medicaid might not cover and she wanted to be able to raise relatively large sums of money quickly and with minimum loss. Alice also thought that inflation was likely to continue at a fairly high level for the foreseeable future and she wanted to protect herself from these pressures as much as possible. These two conditions would suggest short-term investments which would be liquid and provide a return that would move up with inflation.

Third, and most important, Alice wanted her investments to be as safe as possible since the $250,000 was all she would ever have. Alice was no stranger to risk — in the early years of running the business she and her husband had often borrowed every cent they could to meet suppliers' bills. They had always felt they could make up what was lost by working harder. Now, what she lost could not be replaced. Understandably, Alice wanted to keep her risk exposure to a minimum.

Future Lump Sum Requirements

Other than for medical emergencies already mentioned, Alice saw no likelihood of future lump sum payments so that aspect could be ignored. Similarly, since her income needs were fixed, except for the impact of inflation, her strategy need not be influenced by the business cycle. She was not interested in having the estate grow so much as in being able to live securely on the generated income.

Her initial decision, then, was to hold no common stocks at all even though they might have been expected to provide higher returns than other investments she could make.

However, the money market account in her bank was paying only 7.8 percent. If she put her entire portfolio in the account she would only receive $19,500 a year and there would be no adjustment for inflation; clearly that was not going to be adequate for her needs.

An alternative was to put some percentage in long-term U.S. Government Bonds which were paying 12 percent. If she put $125,000 in the long-term bonds and $125,000 in the money market account her situation would be as shown in Table 10.1.

Table 10.1. $125,000 at 7.8% and $125,000 at 12%

Year	Withdrawn	Interest Earned @7.8%	Interest Earned @12%	Ending Balance
0	0	0	0	$250,000
1	22,000	9,750	15,000	252,750
2	22,000	9,965	15,000	255,715
3	22,000	10,196	15,000	258,910
4	22,000	10,445	15,000	262,355
5	22,000	10,714	15,000	266,069
6	22,000	11,003	15,000	270,072
7	22,000	11,316	15,000	274,388
8	22,000	11,652	15,000	279,040
9	22,000	12,015	15,000	284,055
10	22,000	12,406	15,000	289,462
11	22,000	12,828	15,000	295,290
12	22,000	13,283	15,000	301,572
13	22,000	13,773	15,000	308,345
14	22,000	14,301	15,000	315,646
15	22,000	14,870	15,000	323,516
16	22,000	15,484	15,000	332,000
17	22,000	16,146	15,000	341,146
18	22,000	16,859	15,000	351,006
19	22,000	17,628	15,000	361,634
20	22,000	18,457	15,000	373,092

The assumption here is that Alice draws a fixed amount from her money market account, but since the two accounts earn more than $22,000 a year the money market account keeps growing and the interest earned grows as well. However, we have not taken into account the impact of inflation on Alice's needs. If we were to list the amount withdrawn starting with the original $22,000 but growing 6 percent per year, then the situation is less satisfactory (Table 10.2).

Table 10.2. $125,000 at 7.8% and $125,000 at 12%

Year	Withdrawn	Interest Earned @7.8%	Interest Earned @12%	Ending Balance
0	0	0	0	$250,000
1	22,000	9,750	15,000	252,750
2	23,320	9,965	15,000	254,395
3	24,719	10,093	15,000	254,768
4	26,202	10,122	15,000	253,688
5	27,774	10,038	15,000	250,951
6	29,441	9,824	15,000	246,334
7	31,207	9,464	15,000	239,591
8	33,080	8,938	15,000	230,449
9	35,065	8,225	15,000	218,609
10	37,169	7,302	15,000	203,742

Inflation would have increased Alice's needs to $27,775 in the fifth year and $37,169 in the tenth. While the portfolio shows some small growth during the first three years, by the fifth year inflationary demands outstrip the ability of the portfolio to maintain a steady income and the portfolio begins to erode to the point where the money market account is in danger of being used up entirely in a vain attempt to provide Alice with her inflating needs for income.

There are two important assumptions built into Table 10.2, but they tend to compensate for each other. The first is that inflation will be a constant 6 percent per year. The second is that the money market will pay 7.8 percent throughout the period. Any error in one of the assumptions will match a nearly equal and compensating error in the other, that is, if inflation were higher than 6 percent the interest rate on the money market would be higher in proportion, and if inflation were lower, one can expect the money market rates of return to be lower, so the result is not likely to be substantially different from what we show here.

Since it is still unsatisfactory, Alice might like to try still a third alternative, with 75 percent or $187,500 in U.S. Bonds and $62,500 in the money market (Table 10.3).

Table 10.3. $62,500 at 7.8% and $187,500 at 12%

Year	Withdrawn	Interest Earned @7.8%	Interest Earned @12%	Ending Balance
0	0	0	0	$250,000
1	22,000	4,875	22,500	255,375
2	23,320	5,294	22,500	259,849
3	24,719	5,643	22,500	263,273
4	26,202	5,910	22,500	265,481
5	27,774	6,083	22,500	266,289
6	29,441	6,146	22,500	265,494
7	31,207	6,084	22,500	262,870
8	33,080	5,879	22,500	258,169
9	35,065	5,512	22,500	251,117
10	37,169	4,962	22,500	241,410

This is a little better in that the ending balance is substantially higher than it was previously, but the direction is definitely down and after just a few more years Alice's money market account will again be exhausted. Further, the compensating effect that money market variable interest has on inflation is much reduced here since the money market represents a much smaller percentage of Alice's total portfolio.

It seems that Alice cannot preserve her portfolio value in the face of inflating income requirements. What is she to do? Actually she has several choices. She could put some portion of her portfolio in common stocks in the expectation that they would increase in value with inflation. The problem with this strategy, however, is that she doesn't want to (and perhaps should not) take on the risks associated with equity investments.

Alternatively, when she begins to see her portfolio decline in value she could sell her home and invest the proceeds in more bonds or money market instruments. The data in Tables 10.2 and 10.3 suggest that this decline will not come for 5 to 10 years in the future and at that time her personal circumstances may be very different from what they are now. At the moment she is quite capable of taking care of herself and her home. In a few years, however, her health may change or she may prefer not to live alone. She might move in with one of her children or to a residential home or a retirement community.

Financial plans must not be engraved in stone. As circumstances change, portfolio strategy must adjust accordingly. In the case of Alice Johnson, it is virtually impossible to anticipate what the situation will be in 5 or 10 years. The best advice would be to invest as we have suggested above and reexamine the situation — both personal and in the economy around her — in 5 years.

Chapter 11

Case VI
A Small Business
Pension Fund

Pension and profit sharing plans offer a substantial tax advantage to employees and provide employers with a useful way to attract and keep valuable employees. Money paid into these funds is a tax deductible expense to the company just as any wage or salary payment is. However, the employees pay no tax on this income until they actually receive the cash. This would be when they quit the company or retire. At that time they can expect to be taxed at a lower rate. While they remain employed, therefore, employees effectively have a nest egg growing with money—and returns on the money—that is not reduced by taxes.

How should the money in such a fund be invested so that the employees get the greatest benefit? This is exactly the question faced by Harry Jones, president and principal shareholder of Jones & Associates.

Jones & Associates is a five-employee firm which writes computer programs. Harry Jones is 38 years old. One employee, aged 46, is the office manager and accountant. Two programmers are in their twenties. The fifth employee is Harry's brother-in-law, aged 35, who is responsible for new business development.

Three years ago Harry got a contract from a bank to write a special-purpose computer program. With the contract in hand, Harry decided to go into business. He hired a programmer to help him with the detailed programming, and on satisfactory completion of the first contract, was able to get several other jobs from other banks and insurance companies. But Harry saw the severe limitations that custom software imposes on growth and so he set his staff to writing programs for the personal computer market in addition to the contract work.

To attract capable employees to his little company, Harry knew he must offer not only a congenial work environment and interesting work, but a pay and benefit package that was more generous than what they could get elsewhere. Shortly after he landed his second contract, Harry established a profit sharing plan for himself and his employees. Under the provisions of the plan, the company can contribute up to 15 percent of the wages and salaries of all of company employees each year. This year Harry decided to contribute $26,000 which would bring the total amount in the plan to $100,000. Until now the money had been held in a bank Certificate of Deposit, but Harry thought the fund was large enough now to be invested in other instruments such as bonds or equities as well.

**Current
Income
Liquidity
Requirements** Jones & Associates was essentially a young person's company and was likely to remain so for some time. The oldest employee would not retire for at least 15 years and there were no major cash demands likely in the immediate future. Nor was liquidity a requirement unless an employee were to leave the firm and any such payment could probably be covered by the profit contributions made in that year.

Like many other such funds, the profit sharing plan had as its primary objective what fund managers like to call "maximum capital appreciation" within the risk limitations imposed by prudent management. Harry and the two other trustees of the fund had to decide on the proportion of stocks, bonds, and Treasury Bills and whether these proportions should be changed from time to time. Harry discussed the matter with the bank account manager who had sold him the Certificate of Deposit and the manager recommended a ratio of 60 percent equity and 40 percent long-term bonds. His reasoning was that while stocks have a greater growth potential (and so they should be given a larger share of the portfolio), they were inherently more volatile. If the portfolio held some long-term bonds they would not only pay a steady high return but they would take the sting out of those periods when the market turned downward.

The two other trustees of the funds — the firm's lawyer and the accountant — agreed with the bank manager. They thought that for safety's sake the fund should be invested in a diversified portfolio of high quality common stocks and a somewhat smaller amount in long-term bonds.

Stage of the Business Cycle

Harry wasn't convinced that a fixed 60/40 ratio of stocks to bonds was wise. He acknowledged that no matter how careful he was in selecting stocks, some would fall in price and that this might disturb the employees far more than a relatively slow growth in fund value would. Harry thought some change in the proportions, however, during different stages of the business cycle, might improve performance substantially. He decided to test his feeling by comparing two investment strategies. The first was to hold 60 percent of the fund in stocks. The second was to vary the proportions depending on the stage of the business cycle.

In setting up the test he made three basic assumptions:

1. Each portfolio would start at a value of $100,000 and the test would run for five years. To keep things simple, he would include no contributions to the fund other than those earned by dividends and interest on the money previously invested.

2. Returns would vary with the business cycle according to the very rough gauge given in Table 11.1. Harry was quick to admit that it would be difficult to predict exactly when one was at the bottom, midpoint, or top of the cycle, but errors in timing would not substantially affect the levels of return.

Table 11.1. Returns on the three instruments

Instrument	Bottom	Rising	Top	Falling
	Percent of Return			
T Bills	6.0	8.4	10.8	8.4
Stocks	24.0	12.0	−6.0	12.0
Bonds	10.0	11.0	11.5	11.0

3. The fixed portfolio would hold 60 percent stocks, 40 percent long-term bonds. The variable portfolio would be divided among stocks, bonds, and Treasury Bills

depending on the stage of the business cycle. Harry decided to use the proportions recommended for the average investor that were presented in Table 4.1. For convenience we repeat them in Table 11.2

Table 11.2. Portfolio proportions in percent

Stage	T Bills	Stocks	Bonds
At the bottom	5%	75%	20%
Midpoint going up	35	50	15
At the top	70	10	20
Midpoint going down	25	25	50

Fixed vs Variable Portfolio

Harry calculated the value of the variable portfolio after four years with one year in each of the four stages — bottom, rising, top, falling — and then compared it to the value of the fixed portfolio over the same period (Tables 11.3 and 11.4). Since he was covering the full cycle it would not matter when it started.

Table 11.3. Fixed portfolio

Year	Stage	Stocks	Bonds	Total
0		60,000	40,000	100,000
1	Bottom	74,400	44,000	118,400
2	Rising	83,328	48,840	132,168
3	Top	78,328	54,457	132,785
4	Falling	87,728	60,447	148,175

Table 11.4. Variable portfolio

Year	Stage	T Bills	Stocks	Bonds	Total
1 Start	Bottom	5,000	75,000	20,000	100,000
1 End		5,300	93,000	22,000	120,300
2 Start	Rising	42,105	60,150	18,045	120,300
2 End		45,642	67,368	20,030	133,040
3 Start	Top	93,128	13,304	26,608	133,040
3 End		103,186	12,506	29,668	145,360
4 Start	Falling	36,340	36,340	72,680	145,360
4 End		39,393	40,701	80,675	160,769

Harry concluded he could earn more for his employees (and for himself since he was the largest beneficiary of the plan) if he exercised some judgment about the proportions to hold in the three instruments. In fact he could improve the value of the portfolio by $12,000 for every $100,000 invested simply by moving into and out of the various instruments depending on the stage of the business cycle.

Harry was certainly no economist or financial wizard, but the columnists and newsletter writers didn't seem to be all that good at forecasting highs and lows either. He did think he could tell the difference between prosperity and depression and that he could tell when the economy was recovering and when it was declining — and that was all he needed to make his system work.

Chapter 12

Stock Selection Strategies

Up to this point we have concentrated on determining the proportion of your portfolio to be held in equities, Treasury Bills, and bonds. We now turn to the question, which among the thousands of stocks offered on the various markets should you buy?

There are almost as many approaches to this question as there are investors; the problem is that every one of the strategies works well at one time or another. We suspect this is true more because of luck than because of some inherent excellence in the technique. We will discuss a few of the most popular methods and then suggest a combination which is both rational and relatively easy to pursue.

The Industry Approach

Specific industries will experience substantial growth for limited periods of time. At one point the smokestack industries — steel, paper, and machine tool manufacturers — did very well while high-technology companies lagged. At other times the high-technology companies had tremendous growth and profits while the smokestack industries were in the doldrums. Pharmaceutical companies, oil companies, airlines, food manufacturers, home computers, all have their day in the sun and then fall on more difficult times and lose their appeal to investors.

Part of the reason for this popularity is based on performance — the market for the products produced by the industry may suddenly explode and the companies serving the market then scramble to supply the market and make a lot of money in the process.

65

Another part of the reason for such popularity, however, is in the minds of investors whose beliefs about the industry may have little or no relationship to its earnings. This popularity is contagious and suddenly the industry becomes the darling of the market advisors and the "in" group. Stock prices climb to astronomical price/earnings ratios and a lot of money is made — until the bubble bursts, the stock goes out of fashion, and those investors who didn't get out fast enough pay the piper.

The difficulty with using the industry approach in selecting stocks is that you can never be sure which industry will be in favor and, even more important, for how long.

The Random Walk Theory

Another approach starts with the premise that it doesn't make any difference which stocks you buy because variations in stock price are essentially random in nature. Any effort in making thoughtful and considered selections, according to this theory, is wasted.

There is nothing in this theory that says you couldn't have done very well by buying Chrysler at $4 a share in 1982 and selling it at $35 in 1983. Rather, the argument is that there is no publicly available data that an investor might use that would consistently lead to the discovery of a such an opportunity. If an investor were, indeed, to find an approach that worked, it would eventually become common knowledge. Everyone would use the technique and rush to buy the most attractive stocks. The prices for these stocks would quickly rise and thus they would no longer offer the potential for high return on investment.

The random walk approach makes sense up to a point. There is an enormous amount of information available to the investment community in the form of books, magazines, newspapers, newsletters, research reports, business statements, government reports. There are strict regulations about "insider" trading, so that few individual investors are likely to have private information that would allow them to profit at the expense of the market as a whole. But the random walk theory gives investors a little more credit than perhaps it should. It puts more faith in the intelligence and education of investors than the record would justify. Investors do not rush out to adopt successful stock selecting strategies any more than they beat a path to the door of the inventor of the better mousetrap.

 A Fish Tale

Buck Perry is to fishing enthusiasts what Arnold Palmer is to golfers. Buck developed a system that he calls "structure fishing." Buck tells about a visit to a part of the country which was new to him. He stopped at the local bait shop and was told by the owner that a nearby lake was fished out and it would not be worth his time to fish there. Buck rented a boat and after only a few hours on the lake caught his limit. The owner of the bait shop was amazed and the next day went out with Buck to see how he did it.

Instead of casting toward the shoreline, as the bait shop owner suggested, Buck trolled a collection of lures he had designed. By bumping his lures along the lake bottom Buck was able to locate the discontinuities in the bottom that the fish would follow when they move up from their deep water homes to feed in shallower waters. Buck quickly found the fish and again caught his limit.

When they tied up at the dock and were cleaning and wrapping their catch, Buck asked the owner of the shop if he wanted to buy some of the lures that enabled him to map the lake bottom. The owner reflected for a moment and the shook his head. "Nope," he said, "We don't fish that way here."

The fact is that most people neither fish, nor buy stocks, in the most promising waters, and since they don't there is an opportunity for investors to do well if they are willing to take a little time to map the bottom.

Two general principles should be kept in mind. First, you invest in stocks because they offer a higher potential return than a Treasury Bill or a corporate bond. Second, stocks entail higher risk. Investment in a specific stock may not earn as much as you had hoped; its market price may not go up and there is a good chance the price will actually decline. Every investor in the stock market will experience some losses. It is only necessary that the losses be less than the gains. What you want to develop is a strategy for selecting stocks such that the odds of getting a high return are high and the odds of suffering a loss are small.

We'll take a look at the two most successful approaches to selecting stocks and then distill some generalized strategic rules.

Growth Stocks

One technique dear to the investment community is to buy what are called **growth** stocks, meaning stocks whose anticipated earnings and prices climb faster than the average. Surely you have friend or relative who bought IBM or K-Mart or Eastman Kodak for a small sum twenty-five years ago and is now retired and living on a boat in Florida. These were the growth stocks of the 1950s and 1960s. Which are the growth stocks of the 1980s?

Growth stocks have several characteristics in common:

1.   They are leaders in a growing industry, such as IBM in computers.

2.   They are usually technological or marketing pioneers such as McDonald's in the fast food industry or Humana in health care.

3.   They introduce a steady procession of new products and the new products represent a high percentage of total sales. Minnesota Mining, Proctor and Gamble, Baxter Travenol, and Eastman Kodak are such companies.

4.   Their management teams are respected as talented professionals.

5.   They seem to be better able than most companies to earn high profits on the funds they have available to them.

Growth companies are not all as large or as well known as the ones mentioned above. Many small companies have these same characteristics. If a company has at least four of the five characteristics, then these companies will probably do very well for their shareholders over the next few years.

But keeping track of the new product announcements, market developments, and managerial changes of the thousands of companies whose shares are traded is a monumental task. Even the largest brokerage firms, with very strong research departments, can watch only a small number. How can an individual hope to cope?

You do it in a different way. A true growth situation can be determined from a company's financial statements. In essence you compare the return that the company makes for itself (and, therefore, for its shareholders) on the funds it has available to it with the return you could earn by investing the funds elsewhere. By return we mean the ratio of profits to the funds that the shareholders have invested in the company.

Consider your investment alternatives. You could put your money in Treasury Bills — suppose they are currently paying 9 percent interest. This is our no-risk investment (see Appendix B for a further discusson of risk and return). You could invest in 12 percent long-term corporate bonds. The bonds are more risky than the Treasury Bills.

You would certainly not invest in a stock whose return would be less than 9 percent because you could always put your money in the no-risk Treasury Bills and earn that return. You might also expect your investment in a stock to return better than 12 percent because the risk of owning a stock is bound to be greater than that in owning a long-term bond. Suppose that, given the prevailing return on Treasury Bills and corporate bonds that you set 15 percent as your target return on equities.

If a company has a demonstrated history of earning a higher return on its shareholder funds than prevailing interest rates, it has one important attribute of a growth company. A second attribute is the ability to continue to earn that high return in the years to come. In other words it must be able to reinvest a part of the profits it earns so as to create a continuing growth in profits.

Many companies are capable of investing or reinvesting funds at their disposal but they do not have a demonstrated history of earning a high rate of return on the funds they have already invested. Perhaps they are new companies and have no history at all that can be relied on to gauge future performance; perhaps they are entering a new stage in their lives when the potential for explosive growth suddenly appears. Such companies must be categorized as speculative investments, not true growth companies. You are betting on the ability of the management to do something in the future that it has not demonstrated its ability to do in the past.

Other companies may have a history of earning a high return on the funds at their disposal but have only limited opportunities for investing additional funds at a similar return. An example would be the operator of a single gold mine. While the mine may be highly profitable, it will eventually become exhausted. Since there is no direct opportunity for continued investment in the mine, it does not represent a growth situation even though it was highly profitable for its investors.

A growth company, then, is one that has a demonstrated history of earning a high return on an expanding base. As a result, reported profits per share increase year after year at a fast pace. The price of such a company's stock is driven by its demonstrated capacity to earn profits. As profits expand, the stock price is likely to rise.

Undervalued Stocks

A second strategy popular among investors and money managers is to invest in what is termed an "undervalued" stock. We examine the company's balance sheet and, based on calculations which we will describe shortly, determine the true value of the company. If the market price is lower than the true value we categorize the company as undervalued and buy its shares in the expectation that when other investors discover the true value of the company they will bid up the price of its shares until the prices will have risen to the true value.

The problem here is in the calculation of the true value. You must look at the balance sheet which lists many assets such as plant and equipment, inventory of materials, inventory of unsold products, accounts receivable (money owed the company by customers), and so on. Are these assets valued at their proper level? If the equipment were sold tomorrow would it really bring in the value that it is listed at? Could the unsold inventory of products be sold for the value listed? Once a true value of the assets has been established you subtract the liabilities owed by the company — to suppliers, banks, payroll, and so on. The difference is the book value. Divide this by the number of shares outstanding and you have a book value per share which you can compare to the market price.

The key elements to watch for in this calculation are:

1.   Are the accounts receivable (money owed by customers) and the inventories (value of products not yet sold) fairly valued or does the balance sheet overstate their true value? Will some part of the accounts receivable prove uncollectable from customers who will never pay? Are some of the products in inventory obsolete, shopworn, or even nonexistent?

2.   Are the plant and equipment worth the values shown on the balance sheet or are they really worth less or possibly more? Many firms, particularly those that have been in business for a number of years, have already written off (taken off their list of assets) such equipment. But this equipment could still be sold on the second hand market and so the real assets of such a company would actually be higher than the balance sheet suggests.

3.   There is a line on the balance sheet for something called "good will." This is supposed to represent the fair value of the name of the company or its relationships with customers or suppliers that it has taken time to build. This and other such intangible assets may have no value at all if the company were to go out of business and perhaps should be deducted from the book value.

4.   The company may be a poor value if it has a high percentage of short-term debt and the assets that can be quickly converted to cash (like accounts receivable) are not enough to pay off the debt when it falls due.

5.   Is the company's long-term debt so large that the interest on that debt substantially reduces profits which might be invested in new growth opportunities?

To summarize, many professional investment managers consider a company to be undervalued if its market price is less than its book value. If they are conservative they will exclude the value of good will and other intangibles from the stated value of the firm's assets. They will also want to be certain that the debt carried by the company is not so burdensome as to interfere with future operations.

The two approaches described above are based on financial and other data taken from the company's annual report. Each emphasizes a different aspect of the company —the first looks at the demonstrated earning power of the company and its prospects for future earnings; the second focuses on the value of its assets and the relationship between that value and the market price.

1. The earnings approach concentrates on the profit and loss statement which provides information about sales and costs incurred in the last year. The asset approach concentrates on the balance sheet which lists what the company owns and what it owes.

2. The earnings approach is concerned about what products or services the company offers and the markets to which it offers them. The asset approach is concerned with the value of the company's bricks and mortar and how they were financed.

Estimating Value

Let's first define a few business terms we'll be using to be sure we understand each other. **Sales** are the dollars actually received by a company in exchange for its goods or services after all discounts, commissions, etc. **Costs** include all the expenses relating to the running of the company as well costs of materials and labor that go into the products or services. **Profits** are the difference between sales and costs.

A company has a number of different **assets**. They include the money in the corporate bank account, the value of the factory and the land on which it stands, the machines and equipment inside, the money owed to the company by customers (accounts receivable), inventory, etc. In other words, assets are the accumulation of everything of value owned and managed by the company.

Liabilities are the accumulation of all the company's debts — these might include a mortgage on the factory or the land, loans from banks or from private investors in the form of bonds, unpaid bills from materials or components suppliers, taxes due but not yet paid, etc.

The **book value** of a company is its assets minus its liabilities. It is, therefore the **net worth** of the company and is the **equity** that the stockholders share.

Book value is, therefore, the primary interest of those who use the assets approach to stock valuation. The book value divided by the number of shares outstanding is the book value per share. If the book value per share is higher than the current market price per share, then the market is valuing the assets of the company at less than the company spent to acquire them.

The **rate of return** that a company earns on its book value or equity is the ratio of profits to book value expressed as a percent. You find the profits and the book value in the financial reports of a company, divide the one by the other, multiply by 100, and thus calculate a rate of return. It is also sometimes useful to split the rate of return into three components as follows:

$$\frac{\text{Profits}}{\text{Equity}} = \frac{\text{Profits}}{\text{Sales}} \times \frac{\text{Sales}}{\text{Assets}} \times \frac{\text{Assets}}{\text{Equity}}$$

or, in words:

Return on Equity =
Profit Margin × Asset Turnover × Leverage

Each of the three components on the right side of the equation tells us something about how well the company is managed and so we will look at each in some detail.

Profits after taxes divided by sales is called the **Profit Margin**
profit margin. The higher the profit margin, the higher the return on equity will be—all other things being the same. A company will have high profit margins because:

1.   It sells a unique product or service. New and unusual products can command higher prices than older, established products which may have many competitors.

2.   It is a dominant firm in its industry. The company with the largest share of a market can usually produce at the lowest cost because of the efficiencies of high volume production. Thus, the dominant firm usually makes higher profits at the same price or can offer customers equivalent quality at lower prices yet still make the same profit per unit.

3.   It offers something unique to the customer, whether service, product quality, or advertising, so the customer is willing to pay a higher price. If a product is nearly identical to that of its competitors the product becomes a commodity like salt or construction lumber, and then lower prices will be the only way to attract customers away from competitors. Low prices shrink profit margins.

Asset Turnover

The ratio of sales to total assets is called the **asset turnover.** This is a measure of how many times the total dollar assets of the company are sold in a year. An efficient company has a high asset turnover; an inefficient one has a lower asset turnover, though these levels will be different in different industries. A steel mill, with millions of dollars in plant and equipment, will have a lower asset turnover than an architectural design firm whose total assets consist of a few drafting tables, desks, and typewriters. Emphasizing the desirability of high asset turnover may seem unfair to such capital intensive industries, but we are not investing to be fair; we are seeking the highest return possible on our money and capital intensive industries, by definition, require more investment and may produce proportionately lower returns for this investment than do other industries.

Asset turnover can be further split into components that are watched closely by the investment community. As we mentioned earlier, total assets are the sum of accounts receivable, inventory, real estate, plant and equipment, and so on. A high ratio of sales to the inventory component of assets tells us that the company does not tie up its cash (*our* cash) in inventory which just sits on shelves or in warehouses but keeps the inventory small while sales continue at a good clip.

A high ratio of sales to the receivables component of assets indicates that the company can generate cash quickly. It can pay its bills with these funds and won't have to raise cash by incurring additional debt or issuing new stock. A company that collects its bills more slowly is, in effect, lending money to its customers at zero interest. That money is not being put to work to earn a return for the company or its stockholders.

Leverage

The assets of a company include production equipment, the factory, the real estate on which it stands, accounts receivable, inventory, and so on. These assets are purchased either with borrowed funds (debt) or shareholders' investment (equity). If you divide the value of the assets by the value of the equity you get a measure of how much the company relies on its shareholders to fund its its operations and, by extension, how much the company relies on debt. This measure is called the **leverage**. If the leverage is low (near 1.0) the company depends almost entirely on its shareholders to pay for its assets—it is operated in a very conservative way. If the leverage is high (above 3.0) the company depends heavily on debt to finance its operations—a more aggressive and a riskier strategy.

If a company uses debt to buy its plant, equipment, and to pay for the materials it turns into inventory, and if it can produce a higher return on these borrowed funds than it must pay the lenders, then its profits and return on equity will increase. However, the debt will have to be repaid, and a firm with a heavy load of debt may find it has to use almost all of its earnings to repay past borrowings, leaving little to finance the development of new products or new capacity.

Note that it takes time for new products to become profitable. If a firm has high interest payments due on its debt, profits may be sharply reduced or even disappear while the new products are in their introductory stages, and then increase dramatically when the new products achieve acceptance and success. The company may find itself reporting wild swings in earnings—a practice that does not generate confidence among investors who much prefer their company to show steady, and steadily increasing, earnings.

Valuing a Stock

The distinguishing features of an undervalued stock are that its book value is greater than its market price and/or that its rate of return on stockholder's investment (the equity) is greater than the return these same investors could earn by investing their money elsewhere. A measure, then, of how the market as a whole evaluates a particular stock is the ratio of the market price of a share of stock to the equity or book value per share. The relationship is expressed as:

$$\frac{\text{Market Price}}{\text{Book Value}} = \frac{\text{Return on Equity}}{\text{Return on Comparable Investment}}$$

The equals sign here should be interpreted to mean "approaches" or "is driven toward" rather than a strict equality because it is the amount of variance from equality that will represent investment opportunity.

Suppose the management of a company reports that it will be earning 15 percent on its book value this year while you could earn only 10 percent in an alternative investment of comparable risk. Since the return on equity is 1.5 times the return on the comparable alternative investment, we would expect that the market price should be 1.5 times the company's book value. If the book value per share of this company is $20, we would expect the market price to be 1.5 times as large or $30. In other words, if a company's return on equity is greater than the investor's return on a comparable investment elsewhere, the market price of the stock should eventually rise to the point where it is comparably larger than the book value. Conversely, if the return on equity is less than the return on comparable investments elsewhere, the market price will fall to the point that it is proportionately lower than the book value.

This stock valuation is essentially static. It takes the current market price, book value, and so on, without consideration of how these factors may change in the future. In fact a company's earnings will change. If it is successful it will produce profits which may be distributed as dividends and be used to increase the assets and the sales so as to produce still higher profits in the future. As a result the shareholders' equity in the company will increase in time as the stock price can be expect to rise.

If we are to recognize that investors buy a stock not only for its current earnings but its expected future earnings as well, the equation becomes:

$$\frac{\text{Market Price}}{\text{Book Value}} = \frac{\text{Return on Equity}}{\text{Return on Comparable Investment less Expected Growth}}$$

The expected growth is factored into the equation by reducing the return on comparable investment. A company with a high expected growth rate will therefore command a higher market price than one with a lower expected growth rate.

Investors who look for growth opportunities will concentrate on the right side of this equation. They look for companies that have a high return on equity and expect that return to remain high or go higher still.

Investors who look for undervalued stocks concentrate on the left side of this equation. They look for companies whose market price is lower than their book values.

A Strategic Framework

The relationship between these factors—market price, book value, return on equity, return on comparable investment, and expected growth—give us a framework for thinking about which stocks to buy.

In Figure 12.1 a rectangle is divided horizontally by the ratio of return on equity to the return on alternative investments less expected growth. It is divided vertically by the ratio of market price to book value. All companies can be placed in one of the four quadrants.

Figure 12.1. Return map

Market Price / Book Value	Greater Than 1.0	Potential Growth Stock	Over Valued Stock
1.0	Less Than 1.0	Potential Undervalued Stock	Candidate for Change in Management

Greater Than 1.0 $\qquad$ 1.0 $\qquad$ Less Than 1.0

Return on Equity

Return on Comparable Investment

Companies in the upper left quadrant are potential growth stocks. They earn a high return on their equity and the market has recognized their potential by bidding up their price. If the company can maintain and increase profits the market price may continue to rise. Selecting stocks in this quadrant can yield very high returns, however, if the company's return on equity falls, investors will suffer sharp losses because they paid a high price for the company's assets. These companies may have a low business risk (because their profits are high), but they have a high market risk (because their price is high).

Companies in the lower left quadrant appear to be undervalued. As long as earnings are maintained, their price is likely to increase until the two sides of the equation become equal. Such stocks are very appealing because they have both low market risk (their price is low) and low business risk (their profits are high).

Of course, stocks whose prices are below their book values do not always rise in price. The two ratios can approach each other when the rate of return falls. To avoid this possibility we would prefer to invest only in companies whose earnings are currently improving.

Companies in the upper right quadrant are overvalued. So long as this is true there is a substantial risk that the price will fall so as to bring the two ratios together. Companies in this quandrant have both high business risk and high market risk. Of course if profits rise and the rate of return begins to rise, the downward pressure on the market price will disappear.

Companies in the lower right quadrant are in serious trouble and may need either a change in management or a change in operating policy, or both. The management is not using the assets it controls to produce as high a return for shareholders as they can get elsewhere. The market recognizes these failings and has driven the price down accordingly.

The return map shown in Figure 12.1 provides a good framework for strategic analysis. It pinpoints the type of data you will need and provides a clear measure of the stocks you are considering buying. By disciplining yourself to set standards and select only those stocks that meet the standards, you can be sure you are fishing in the most promising waters.

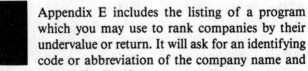

A Stock Valuation Program

Appendix E includes the listing of a program which you may use to rank companies by their undervalue or return. It will ask for an identifying code or abbreviation of the company name and then for the following data:

1. Company name (8 characters or less)
2. Current market price per share

3. Book value per share
4. Total sales
5. Total assets
6. Total equity
7. Total profits
8. Return on comparable investment

All these data can be found in the annual reports issued by companies or in one of the many security references such as *Value Line, Standard and Poor* or *Moody's*. The program will produce a table as follows:

Table 12.1.   Stocks ranked by ROE/ROCI ratio

Stock	$ Market Price	$ Book Value	% Prof/ Sales	% Sales/ Assets	% Assts/ Equity	Price/ Book	ROE/ ROCI	Quad
DEF	29.25	32.25	16.7	150.0	100.0	0.907	2.500	2
JKL	42.25	55.00	10.0	600.0	33.3	0.768	2.500	2
ZZZ	12.00	10.00	20.0	250.0	40.0	1.200	2.000	1
PQR	13.25	20.00	20.0	200.0	50.0	0.663	1.667	2
GHI	15.50	10.00	8.3	50.0	100.0	1.550	0.521	3
CCC	9.50	6.00	5.0	200.0	100.0	1.583	0.500	3
ABC	51.00	60.00	10.0	40.0	250.0	0.850	0.500	4
MNO	86.25	50.00	10.0	20.0	200.0	1.725	0.364	3

Quadrants are: 1 — Potential growth stock
                 2 — Potential undervalued stock
                 3 — Overvalued stock
                 4 — Needs change in management

Stocks are ranked by the ratio of Return on Equity to Return on a Comparable Investment. This establishes whether the stocks are in quadrants 1 or 2 (ratio above 1.0), or quadrants 3 or 4 (ratio below 1.0).

Chapter 13

Option Selection Strategies

What we really want for our investment portfolio is the highest possible return at the least risk. The problem is that risk and return tend to move together—you cannot ordinarily increase your return without also increasing your risk—so if you invest in instruments which promise high returns you are likely to find that they entail a higher risk of loss.

Of the three investment instruments we have been considering—money market instruments, bonds, and stocks—stocks offer the highest return and the highest risk. For example, when you buy a stock you do so in the expectation that you will get good returns from dividends and from increase in stock price. However, you risk the possibility that the dividends will be lower than expected or the price of the stock may not increase or it may actually decline.

Options are another means of speculating in the price of stocks but, by the nature of the option, they offer a higher potential return on your investment—and substantially higher risk.

To understand option trading let's first review the essentials of short-term stock trading: You can buy a hundred shares of stock, hold them for a period and then sell them. If the stock increases in price you profit by the increase less the commissions or other fees taken by the stockbroker. Alternatively, you can sell a hundred shares of stock (even if you don't own them—in effect you borrow them from your stockbroker temporarily) and then later buy them back. If the stock price drops during the period between the sale (at the higher price) and the repurchase (at the lower price), you profit by the difference, less the broker's commissions.

Profits in short-term trading, then, are dependent on the movement of the stock price. If you buy and the stock price rises you show a profit; if you sell and the stock price falls you show a profit. When you trade in options you are similarly dependent on the price of the stock, but the stock itself may never change hands — you are exchanging a *promise* to buy or sell the stock if, during a given period of time, its price moves past a predetermined level.

Suppose it is June and you have just sold a small summer cottage that has been in your family for many years. After deducting all commissions and real estate fees you find yourself with $10,500 that you wish to invest. You glance through the stock listings and note that IBM is selling at $105 a share and so, stockbroker's commissions aside, you can buy 100 shares of IBM with your money.

Now IBM is a well-run company and it is currently enjoying a lot of success in the small computer market. It is also a very large company and the target of many smaller, highly competitive ones, which delight in introducing new products that may be considered technologically superior to IBM's. Thus IBM's profits and growth, and its stock price, could easily decline. But let's suppose you really believe in this company and are convinced that it is very unlikely that the stock will decline in price.

You can buy the stock with your $10,500 and earn the profits indicated in Table 13.1.

Table 13.1. Stock profits on IBM shares

If the stock price goes to	Your gross profits or losses are
$130	$2,500
125	2,000
120	1,500
115	1,000
110	500
105	0
100	− 500
95	− 1,000
90	− 1,500

But rather than buying the 100 shares of IBM outright you note that you can buy an October IBM call option at 110 for $5.

A call option is the right, should you choose to exercise it, to buy a specified stock from the seller of the option at a specified price for a limited period of time. The price at which you can buy the stock, $110 in this case, is called the striking price; this is the price at which the seller agrees to sell the stock should you choose to exercise your option. The right to buy is yours from the moment of purchase of the call option until the expiration month—in this case October. Options are sold in 100 share lots, so to buy one such call would actually cost you $500 plus broker's commissions.

Note several interesting things about this agreement. First, the seller doesn't actually have to own the stock. The seller has simply agreed to sell you shares at $110 a share at any time between now and October. It will be his responsibility to buy the shares if necessary— at whatever price, if you choose to exercise the option. Obviously it would make no sense for you to exercise the option and actually buy the shares unless the price has gone above $110. If it stays below $110, or even reaches that level, you have got nothing for your pains since you could yourself as easily buy the shares on the open market directly. In fact, since you have paid $5 per share for the option, you don't stand to profit by the agreement unless the stock price goes above $115 per share. Then you could buy the shares at $110 each, and immediately sell them at the higher market price and get your $5 investment back.

If the price does not go above $110 between June and October, your call is worthless. The option expires and you have lost $500. If the price goes above $110 but below $115 it may pay to exercise the option and sell the stock so that you get at least part of your $5 investment back. For example, suppose the stock rises to $113. If you exercise the option and buy the stock at $110 you can immediately resell it for the current price of $113 and net $3 per share. Take commissions out and you may still have a small profit—though you haven't recouped the $5 per share investment that the option cost in the first place.

Let's say you took the entire $10,500 and invested it in these calls. That means you would have bought calls on 2,100 shares of stock ($10,500/$5 = 2,100) (Table 13.2).

Table 13.2.   Profits on IBM call options

If the stock price goes to	Your gross profits or losses are
$130	$31,500
125	21,000
120	10,500
115	0
110	− 10,500
105	− 10,500
100	− 10,500
95	− 10,500
90	− 10,500

The potential profits are very large while the potential losses are your entire investment. Of course you can arbitrarily limit your risk by investing less. Suppose instead of investing all $10,500 in the IBM calls you decide to invest just enough to achieve profits similar to those you would make if you had actually bought the underlying stock. If you bought calls on 300 shares you would have to invest only $1,500. You could take the other $9,000 and put it in a Treasury Bill.

With calls costing $5 each on 300 shares and a $110 striking price the profits are as shown in Table 13.3.

Table 13.3.   Profits on three IBM call options

If the stock price goes to	Your gross profits or losses are
$130	$4,500
125	3,000
120	1,500
115	0
110	−1,500
105	−1,500
100	−1,500
95	−1,500
90	−1,500

Again we see the higher return possibilities — you can double or triple your investment if the price rises sharply, but if the price only reaches $115 or any level below that, you stand to lose part or all of the $1,500. As a comparison, if you bought the stock itself, the price would have to drop to $90 to make your losses the same.

We have simplified this analysis somewhat to bring out the important points about call options. Specifically we have not discussed how the price of the call option moves as it approaches the expiration date, nor have we related the price of the option to the volatility of the under-lying stock price. We have also not included broker's commissions which have the effect of increasing the price of a call option and therefore requiring a still higher movement in the price of the underlying stock if a profit is to be made. And we have neglected the interest that would be earned if we put the $9,000 in a Treasury Bill.

In any case the message should be clear. Options increase the potential returns of an investment at a com-mensurately higher risk.

Put Options

If buying call options is a high-risk, high-return way of betting that a stock price will rise, the put option is a high-risk, high-return way of betting that a stock price will fall. It is very similar to selling a stock short. Note that in selling a stock short you need not own the underlying stock; you may borrow the stock from your broker, sell it on the market and, when the time seems right, buy it back on the market to return to your broker. If the price has declined between the time you borrowed the stock and returned it, you will have profited by the difference — less broker's commissions.

Suppose you have read an article in a trade journal indicating that a large chemical company which is a close competitor of Monsanto Chemical is about to mount a major sales effort with new sales people, a large adver-tising campaign, and so on. You know, of course, that the price of Monsanto stock depends on a number of factors, including the company's future earnings, its ability to pay dividends, the value of its assets, and such overall market conditions as the movement of interest rates and the general state of the economy.

All things considered, you are convinced that the stock market as a whole will decline and that Monsanto in particular has nothing going for it that would allow its price to move against the market. You decide to use the $10,500 to sell Monsanto short. The first thing you do is call your broker and ask for the current market price of Monsanto. For simplicity let's say it is $50 a share. You tell the broker to sell 100 shares for you. The broker makes the sale and you now have $5,000 in your account, less broker's commissions. However, you owe the broker 100 shares of Monsanto Chemical, so the broker isn't going to let you take all of the $5,000 out of the account in cash and go on a European vacation. Until you have returned those 100 shares most of the money will be retained in the account.

However, after a period of time you go out onto the open market, buy 100 shares of Monsanto, return them to the broker and close out the trade (Table 13.4).

Table 13.4.   Profits on a short sale of Monsanto shares

If the stock price goes to	Your gross profits or losses are
$75	$ – 2,500
70	– 2,000
65	– 1,500
60	– 1,000
55	– 500
50	0
45	500
40	1,000
35	1,500

In buying a put option you buy the right to sell a stock at a set price which may be higher or lower than the current price. Suppose Monsanto put options for October are quoted at $3 per share at a striking price of $50. You buy put options on 3,500 shares for your $10,500. If the price falls to $40 you stand to profit $10 per share less your cost of the options and broker's commissions. That amounts to $10 times 3,500 shares or $35,000 less $10,500, for a net, before commissions, of $24,500 (Table 13.5)!

Table 13.5.   Profits on Monsanto put options

If the stock price goes to	Your gross profits or losses are
$80	$ – 10,500
75	– 10,500
70	– 10,500
65	– 10,500
60	– 10,500
55	– 10,500
50	0
45	7,000
40	24,500

However, just as in the purchase of the call options, you are risking the entire $10,500. If you wanted to be a little more conservative and decided to buy put options for only 500 shares the potential loss is much less serious, and the potential rewards are still substantial (Table 13.6).

Table 13.6.   Profits on 500 Monsanto put options

If the stock price goes to	Your gross profits or losses are
$80	$ – 1,500
75	– 1,500
70	– 1,500
65	– 1,500
60	– 1,500
55	– 1,500
50	0
45	1,000
40	4,500

The potential profit that you can make through either put or call options depends on the volatility of the stock price and the premium that you pay. The more volatile the stock price, the greater the potential gain.

To review: You buy a call option if you think the price of the stock is going to rise sharply; you buy a put option if you think the price of the stock is going to fall sharply. However, these are high-risk, high-return (i.e., highly speculative) investments. You will lose your entire investment if the underlying stock moves only a small amount in the expected direction or if it moves against the expected direction. Further you have only a limited period of time in which the move may take place. You may be correct in your judgment as to the direction and amount of movement, and wrong on the timing, and the result is just as disastrous as if you were wrong on the direction.

Covered Calls

 If you can buy an option, either put or call, some-one must be the seller. Many professional investors write "covered calls" as part of their investment strategy. This means they own the underlying stocks and sell calls against their holdings to earn the premium. Suppose it is early June and you note that Alcoa, whose current price is $34.62, has October $35 calls selling at $2.75. You decide to buy the stock and sell a call against this position.

Your reasoning might go something like this: If the price of Alcoa should fall it will have to go below $31.87 before you will experience any loss — this is the net cost to you of the stock — $34.62 minus the $2.75 you received for the call. Obviously you don't think this is likely otherwise you wouldn't have bought the stock in the first place.

If the price of the stock rises above $35, the call will be exercised by the buyer. Your receipts will be $35 for the stock plus $2.75 for the call for a total of $37.75. Your net profit will be $3.13 per share for a return of 9 percent on the investment (less broker's commissions, of course).

Note that the expiration date is October and the purchase was made in June. You will have earned this 9 percent return in four months (or less if the striking price is reached earlier) for an effective annual rate of return of 27 percent or more. If the striking price is never reached you have pocketed the $2.75 and still own the stock.

The risks in such a strategy are these: First the broker's commissions (transaction charges) can eat up much of the profit. There will be a charge at the initial purchase of the stock and on the sale of the call. If the call is exercised there will be a charge for buying back the call and selling the underlying stock. It would be easy for these four transaction charges to cost as much as the $2.75 sale of the call. The reason professional traders often use this strategy is that they can trade at favorable brokerage rates and keep the transaction charges to a small amount.

Second, if the underlying stock falls sharply you will lose money on the trade and a single bad trade can wipe out the profits of four or five successful trades. Again, professional traders are likely to watch stocks very carefully—the prices they pay, the direction the prices are moving, and the cost of the call—and so a movement in the wrong direction can be reacted to very quickly, before any damage is done.

As we have been describing them, options are a highly speculative investment strategy, but you can also use them to protect a portfolio and therefore function as a kind of insurance policy against potential loss. This is best explained by another example.

Options as Insurance

Suppose you have a carefully selected portfolio of stocks currently worth $50,000. You chose companies with sales over $75 million a year, whose earnings have been consistently rising over the last five years, and companies that financed their capital expenditures out of internally generated sources. You spent a lot of time picking these companies and you believe they will perform as well as if not better than the market as a whole.

The problem is that the economy appears to be approaching a peak. Interest rates are high and seem to be going higher, and you suspect that stock prices are on the verge of turning downward. Good portfolio management strategy suggests that you get out of stocks and into the bond market, but you are reluctant to give up any part of the $50,000 portfolio that you have so carefully built over the years.

Instead you buy some insurance in the form of put options on the Standard & Poor's 100 Stock Index. The Index put is exactly like any other put. At the moment we are considering your portfolio, the Standard & Poor's Index is 150. Available put options with a striking price of 150 are selling for $3.25 or $325 for 100 shares. You buy six such contracts for $1,950.

Now if the stock market as a whole declines by 5 percent, and your portfolio falls by a similar amount, the portfolio has lost $2,500 in value. However, the put options you bought can be sold for $750 each (5% × 150 = $7.50; $7.50 × 100 = $750). Six of them are worth $4,500. Take off the $1,950 you paid for the puts to begin with and you are still $2,550 ahead and the total portfolio is now worth $50,500 ($47,500 + $2,550).

If the stock market as a whole goes up by 5 percent (against your expectations, but still possible), and the portfolio goes up by a similar amount, it will be worth $52,500. But you have paid $1,950 for the six put options and so your net portfolio value is now $50,500.

The effect is to insure you against a downward movement of the market. The cost is the same as in any insurance—when the loss doesn't occur you are out the cost of the insurance. Let's see a range of market changes and how the put options protect you (Table 13.7).

Table 13.7. Options as insurance on a portfolio

If the market change is	A $50,000 portfolio will be worth	Six $150 S&P options are worth	Net value after cost of option
+15%	$57,500	0	$55,550
+10%	55,000	0	53,050
+ 5%	52,500	0	50,550
0	50,000	0	48,050
− 5%	47,500	$ 4,500	50,050
−10%	45,000	9,000	52,050
−15%	42,500	13,500	54,050

It is interesting to note that in this example the effect of buying the put options is to increase the value of the portfolio no matter which way the market goes if it moves by a large enough amount. A large market rise will offset the cost of the put and let the portfolio increase in value. A large price fall will make the value of the put option greater than the portfolio loss. The maximum loss is the cost of the insurance. This occurs when the market neither rises nor falls.

You must decide for yourself whether, and how much, insurance you need. Obviously if you think the market is at the the bottom and rising you will not need to buy any put options. If you think it is at the peak and falling it may be prudent to be fully protected.

Chapter 14

Bond Selection Strategies

Choosing the bonds you buy requires the same thoughtful consideration used in selecting stocks. The elements of bond selection strategy, however, are quite different from those of a stock selection strategy:

1. Interest payments received on bonds issued by state and local governments may be exempt from federal taxes; the interest paid on bonds issued by corporations and the federal government are not.

2. The maturity of a bond — when the company must pay back the face value — can be as short as one year or as long as 20 years or more. However, many bonds have a call feature. This means that the company can buy back the bonds when it chooses though it will have to pay a specified price at each date.

3. Most bonds are relatively risk free in that there is little doubt that the borrower (the seller of the bond) will pay off the maturity value when due. However, some companies may have trouble meeting their interest and principal amounts on a timely basis. The more risky the bond, the higher the interest rate the company must offer to attract investors. Some bonds have special features such as being able to convert them into common stock. These features influence the rate of interest that will be paid on the bond and its purchase price at the time of offering or later.

Bonds offered by state and local governments are exempt from federal taxes. The reason for this lies deep in the constitutional history of our country. In one of its very early decisions, the Supreme

Taxable vs Nontaxable

Court ruled that if the federal government were permitted to tax the bonds of the states it could destroy the delicate balance that was being established between the rights of states and those of the federal government. Thus, the interest rates on municipal bonds are usually lower than those offered by the federal government, while their after tax rates may be higher. A federal bond might be offered at 12 percent interest while a state bond might be offered at 7 percent. If an investor were in the 50 percent tax bracket, the 7 percent return is equivalent to a pretax return of 14 percent.

There are two major types of tax exempt bonds. The first is a general obligation of the issuing organization. The full faith and credit of the community stands behind these bonds. In other words, the community pledges that it will levy suffient taxes upon its citizens or in some other way raise funds to pay off the bonds when they mature.

The second type is a revenue bond. This is issued to pay for a specific revenue-gathering activity, such as a toll road or an industrial park, and the revenues of the project are pledged to meet the interest payments and the principal, when due. However, if the revenues are not sufficient, the community has no further obligation and the investor may not be repaid in full. Revenue bonds are therefore considered riskier investments than the general obligation bonds.

Tax exempt bonds have a place in the portfolios of investors who are in a high tax bracket and who are interested in current income more than overall growth of their portfolios. If the investor is in a lower tax bracket the case for tax exempt bonds is less compelling.

Maturity Bonds have different maturities and a successful investment strategy will make use of this fact. We have already noted how interest rates fluctuate over the business cycle, and that it is difficult to predict exactly when the peak or trough of a cycle will occur.

Suppose you plan to hold $50,000 in bonds in your portfolio. You are concerned that if you buy a single bond you will lock yourself into an interest rate that is appropriate for today but may turn out to be lower than you can get next year or the year after. You reduce the risk of bad timing by spreading the maturity of the bonds you buy.

You might purchase $10,000 in a bond that matures at the end of year 1; $10,000 in a bond that matures at the end of year 2; and so on for each of the next five years. Now when the first bond comes to maturity you reinvest the proceeds in a bond that matures five years later. At the end of year two you do the same thing with the proceeds from that sale. If you do this every year for the five years you will hold a total of $50,000 in bonds at all times, as planned, but you have effectively set the interest rate to the average of the five-year period rather than having it locked into the rate prevailing at the time the investment was originally made. Note that this strategy makes no attempt to anticipate the changes in interest rates. It is simply designed to reduce the risk and the range of interest fluctuations.

 Risk

Companies, and even state or local governments, may encounter difficulty in meeting interest or principal payments when they are due. Chrysler Corporation was in serious financial difficulties in the late 1970s; International Harvester and other farm equipment companies and several airline companies had financial problems in the early 1980s.

Any organization is going to have financial problems when earnings decline for a sustained period. As the probability grows that interest payments will not be met, the price of the bond will fall and the yield to the new buyer (if the organization does make its payments when due) will increase.

Two firms rate the riskiness of bonds for investors. These are Standard and Poor, and Moody's. The highest credit rating an organization can have is AAA. An AA rating is a little more risky, A is riskier still, then comes BBB, BB, and so on. The highest risk bonds are rated C.

It takes a good deal of judgment to assess the small differences in probability that an organization will not be able to meet its interest obligations. Some of the factors include:

1. The ratio of the earnings to its interest obligations. If this ratio is high, the firm should not experience any

trouble in paying interest due. As this ratio goes lower, the credit rating of its bonds will fall.

2.   The ratio of cash flow generated by the organization to the interest payments. As this ratio falls, the organization will experience greater difficulty in meeting it obligations. Investors will become concerned about whether they will be paid and will insist on being compensated for the additional risk.

3.   The ratio of total debt to the equity of a corporation. The higher the ratio, the riskier the bonds. In theory, bond holders look at the liquidated value of the corporation's assets as their guaranty that the bond can be paid off. If the ratio of debt to equity is too high, the sale of the corporate assets may not generate enough cash to pay off all of the debt.

The riskiness of a corporation changes over the business cycle. When the economy is prosperous, many firms can generate enough cash to cover their obligations. However, when the economy moves toward recession, earnings can rapidly disappear and the earnings ratio mentioned above will shrink. Astute investors can take advantage of this fact. Suppose a particular company offers B-rated bonds and the economy is in a recession. Because of the poor credit rating the bonds must offer a relatively high yield. As the economy begins to recover, the earnings of the B-rated company improve. The company now has no trouble at all in meeting its interest obligations and its credit rating will improve. The price of the bonds issued during the recession will rise so as to keep the fixed interest payments at an effectively lower rate to the new purchaser. It is wise, therefore, during the early stages of an economic recovery, to buy the bonds of companies with somewhat weaker credit ratings.

Conversely, when the economy is at its peak it is wise to buy bonds with high credit ratings. As the economy moves toward recession these strong companies are likely to maintain their high credit ratings and bond prices, while companies with weaker ratings may be downrated and their bonds will fall in value.

Special Features Convertibility adds a value to a bond that may be very desirable to an investor. For example, suppose you are offered a bond with a $1,000 par value paying 7 percent interest that may be converted into 50 shares of common stock of the company at any time. If the price of the stock rose to $40 a share the bond would be worth at least $2,000. The bondholders could exchange the bond for 50 shares, sell the shares, and pocket $2,000. Indeed, any time the price of the company's stock exceeds $20 a share, the bond will be worth more than the par value of $1,000. If the price of the stock falls below $20, however, the bondholder need not worry about the value of the investment since the 7 percent interest rate is still being paid. In short, when the price of the common stock is high, the convertible bond sells as if it were a stock; if the price of the stock is low, it sells as if it were just a bond.

Convertible bonds are attractive to investors for this very reason. They appear to have great upside potential and a limited amount of downside risk. The disadvantage of convertible bonds is that the investor pays a premium for this feature. Sometimes the premium is so high that it would be better to buy the common stock outright instead of the bond—if price appreciation is the goal, or to buy a standard bond—if steady income is the objective.

Conclusions

The amount of money invested in bonds depends on the investor's need for a steady stream of earnings, the ability to tolerate risk, and the stage of the business cycle. We have spent most of this book helping you establish the percentage of a portfolio to be invested in this way.

Once the amount has been determined the choice between tax-free municipals or corporate bonds depends on the tax bracket—investors in high tax brackets will do better with tax-free state and local bonds because their after tax returns are higher. The manager of a tax exempt fund such as a pension plan or a profit sharing plan will always select a corporate bond since the fund pays no taxes anyway and these bonds offer a higher interest rate.

The decision as to what maturity is more difficult. If a long-term bond is purchased and interest rates rise, the bondholder will lose out on interest that might have been earned. If a short-term bond is purchased and interest rates fall, the bondholder will similarly lose on interest that might have been earned. To avoid the problems of anticipating how interest rates will move, you can spread your purchases among bonds that mature every year for five to seven years and thus assure yourself of at least maintaining a rate equivalent to the average interest for the next five years.

The decision about what credit rating is appropriate depends on your risk tolerance. If the portfolio is limited to AA- or AAA-rated bonds it will be very safe but its yield will be lower than that of a portfolio with somewhat lower rated bonds. In general it is advisable to buy lower rated bonds when the economy is at bottom and higher rated ones when it is at the peak.

Some sophisticated investors can take advantage of special features of bonds. The bond that has specified assets pledged may be a better credit risk than that indicated by the corporation's general credit rating. However, to take advantage of special features of bonds or to shift between credit ratings over the business cycle is quite difficult for all but the most professional investors.

Chapter 15

Money Market Selection Strategies

Highly liquid instruments—investments that may be turned into cash very quickly—have a role to play in every investment portfolio. We will call this general category of investment money market instruments, though such instruments would include a wide variety of money market funds, Certificates of Deposit, or Treasury Bills. In addition to liquidity, these instruments offer reasonable price stability, and they often provide returns nearly equal to (and sometimes better than) those offered by equities and long-term bonds.

Consider the following three fictional investors and how they selected money market instruments to serve specific, and different, requirements for income, liquidity, and safety.

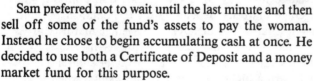

Sam Breen was responsible for his company's pension plan. One of the firm's employees was coming up for retirement and she told Sam that she would want to withdraw all of her accumulated pension in cash.

A Pension Fund

Sam preferred not to wait until the last minute and then sell off some of the fund's assets to pay the woman. Instead he chose to begin accumulating cash at once. He decided to use both a Certificate of Deposit and a money market fund for this purpose.

A Certificate of Deposit is a note issued by a bank. This is one of the ways banks raise money that they then lend to companies or individuals. The investor can negotiate the amount of time the bank will be permitted to keep the money as well as the interest rate that the bank will pay. The terms are fixed during the life of the Certificate of Deposit, which typically matures in six to twelve months, though occasionally for longer periods. Certificates of Deposit cannot be sold before maturity without incurring a penalty so they are somewhat less liquid than other money market instruments, but they are placed in this category because of their short maturity times. Certificates of Deposit are very safe — virtually zero risk — because they are insured by the Federal Deposit Insurance Corporation — effectively the U.S. government.

In contrast with the Certificate of Deposit, the money market fund pays a variable rate of interest and the rate may change daily. Moreover, the money market fund has no fixed maturity. Rather, investors can put money in or take money out of the fund on a daily basis if they choose. However, this liquidity comes at a price; the yield on a money market fund is usually less than that of a Certificate of Deposit. Moreover, the investor's funds are not guaranteed by the government.

There is a wide variety of money market funds to choose from. They offer different services — for example, some permit you to write checks against your account, though the checks usually must be above a specified amount. They also differ in the kinds of assets, and the maturity dates of the assets, they hold. Some funds only invest in U.S. Treasury Bills, others hold bank Certificates of Deposit or short-term obligations of corporations, still others buy only short-term state and local obligations. Some funds buy obligations that have an average maturity of only a few days so the managers are busy turning the fund over and over all the time. Others may have an average maturity of a few weeks. Some modify their average maturity depending on the trend in prevailing interest rates. The difference in average maturity affects the return the fund can earn for its investors. When interest rates are rising, the fund with the shorter maturity will earn a higher rate on its investments; when interest rates are falling the fund with the longer maturity will earn a higher rate.

Sam decided to put the cash contribution normally paid by the company to the pension fund into a Certificate of Deposit that matured on the date the employee would retire. He also put all the dividends earned by the fund's investments, as well as any proceeds from security sales made during this period, into a money market fund. By investing in these two ways he would accumulate enough to fulfill the fund's obligations to the retiring employee and do so with least disruption to the equity and bond purchasing strategy he was using for the fund.

A Retired Woman

Mary Duggan has been managing her 78-year-old mother's portfolio for some time now. Not counting her modest home, the estate is worth about $40,000 and so her mother depends for her living expenses on the money she receives from Social Security added to what the portfolio can earn.

Mary's mother wants to be certain her money is safe at all times and so Mary decides to put the entire portfolio in Treasury Bills and roll it over (reinvest in the same instrument) when the bills mature every six months.

There are some distinct disadvantages to this decision: There is a fee due to the bank or brokerage firm when the Treasury Bills are purchased; Mary could get a higher return for her mother by investing in a Certificate of Deposit; finally, the Treasury Bills will not be quite as convenient as a money market fund would be. But her mother wants to be safe at all costs, and under the circumstances Mary feels she has no choice but to buy the Treasury Bills.

Tax Consequences

Money market funds are mutual funds, which means that when you invest in a money market fund you are actually buying shares of the fund. The fund managers invest this money in short-term, highly liquid assets. After deducting fund operating expenses, all the revenues are passed back to the shareholders of the fund in the form of dividends. The dividends of funds that invest in state and municipal obligations are therefore exempt from federal taxes. It is as if the investor bought a tax-exempt state or local bond issue outright.

Susan Cohn, 56, manages her family's savings. Both she and her husband have relatively high incomes and are in a high tax bracket, so Susan is always concerned about the tax implications of any investment decision she makes. When she contemplates investing in money market instruments she compares the tax-free yield of the municipal or state money market fund against the higher, but taxable, yield of other funds so as to be sure she will earn the highest return on her investment. It turns out that most of the time she is better off investing in the tax-free money market fund.

Note that in all of these examples our investors have used money market instruments to meet specific, but very different, requirements. Sam invested in a Certificate of Deposit as well as a money market fund for safety and convenience. Mary bought Treasury Bills for her mother to be as risk free as possible. Susan found that her after-tax income would be highest with a tax-free money market fund.

Treasury Bills and Open Market Operations

Investors should be aware of a more subtle aspect of Treasury Bills. The U.S. government uses Treasury Bills as a means by which the Federal Reserve controls the country's money supply and interest rates.

Before World War II the amount of Treasury Bills outstanding rarely exceeded $2.5 billion. By 1945, however, the total had risen to over $17 billion as the government borrowed the funds it needed to wage war. By 1984 the total outstanding volume was in excess of $350 billion.

This rapid rise in the volume of Treasury Bills is due, in part, to the large government deficits that have continued under all recent administrations. But deficits are not the only reason. The government could have borrowed using long-term bonds rather than the shorter-term Treasury Bills. Treasury Bills are a popular debt instrument widely sought after by investors both in the United States and abroad. American and foreign banks, pension funds, corporations, and individuals like to hold Treasury Bills because of their safety and liquidity.

Since Treasury Bills are obligations of the federal government, there is no question that they will be paid when due. Moreover, because they are so liquid, an investor need not wait until maturity if cash is needed quickly. Large quantities of bills can be bought or sold without moving the price significantly.

Because Treasury Bills are the safest possible short-term asset one can buy, the interest rate offered is lower than any other asset of comparable maturity. Therefore, when the interest rate on Treasury Bills rises all other short-term rates will increase as well, and when the interest rate on Treasury Bills falls all other rates must come down too.

The Federal Reserve is conscious of this relationship between Treasury Bill rates and other interest rates and will buy or sell Treasury Bills whenever it wants to influence either the amount of money in circulation or the prevailing level of interest rates. When the Federal Reserve wants to tighten credit it will sell Treasury Bills at higher interest rates. This restricts the money supply by soaking up money that would otherwise be in circulation. Conversely, when the Federal Reserve wants to put downward pressure on interest rates and increase the money supply, it will buy back Treasury Bills or reduce the issuance of new ones and this puts money back into the hands of the public and lets the interest rates drift downward.

Many investors have become quite sophisticated about the open market operations of the Federal Reserve. They try to anticipate what action the Federal Reserve will take. For example, they ask themselves, "Is the economy strong?" If the answer is yes, the Federal Reserve can be expected to try to tighten credit to drive up interest rates and curb inflationary pressures. To protect yourself from rising interest rates, you sell stocks and long-term bonds, and invest in highly liquid, short-term instruments.

When the economy is slowing, investors would guess that the Federal Reserve is likely to try to stimulate the economy by buying Treasury Bills. This will increase the money supply and drive down interest rates. This is a good time to buy common stocks and long-term bonds because as rates fall, these other instruments will increase in value.

Chapter 16

How to Monitor Portfolio Performance

In the best of all worlds you will buy a stock, tuck it away in your safety deposit box, and several years later discover that it is worth a fortune. You are rich! You retire and live happily ever after.

Unfortunately, there is no surer way to lose money than to buy a stock and then to forget about it. As we have said time and again in this book, the portfolio must be tuned to the stages of the economy as a whole and to your personal circumstances — both of which are subject to change. Further, individual stocks also experience changes in their fortunes. Some of the changes are related to the health of the company itself and the luck or excellence of its managers' decisions; some are related to the way the company is regarded by the investment community.

Suppose you had set up your portfolio a year ago, when the economy was at the bottom. You put 60 percent in equities, 20 percent in bonds, and 20 percent in the money market. As the economy improved, the equities appreciated in value and today they represent 80 percent of the portfolio with only 7 percent in bonds and 13 percent in the money market. It is clearly time to be making some adjustments — particularly since the economy is almost midway into its rise and the equities may not have much further to go.

The situation is a happy one but not one that will stay happy if neglected. Failing to make the necessary adjustments means that you are no longer in control — all the gains could easily be lost if you allow the portfolio to be governed by chance rather than by your investment strategy.

Or suppose you had decided to limit your equity investments to small companies with relatively low price/earnings ratios, moderate dividend yields, but very good prospects for future earnings. Last year you found a number of such undervalued companies and carefully distributed your portfolio among six of them.

In time, four of the companies did appreciate in value—to the point where the price/earnings ratio was no longer low. The other two reported lower quarterly earnings for three quarters in a row and their stock prices turned downward. It sounds like the time might be approaching to consider selling all six stocks and to reinvest the proceeds in a new set of undervalued stocks. But you wouldn't know that the time had arrived either for the profitable stocks or the losers unless you had done a careful review of the entire portfolio in the light of the current state of the economy, your personal circumstances, and your investment strategy.

We recommend a full-scale formal review at least every three months and preferably once a month—and the portfolio should not be neglected between formal review periods. Many professional investors review their portfolios weekly and keep close watch on specific stocks on a daily basis.

The formal review takes an investment of time, attention, and energy, and in the interests of making this investment as efficient as possible we feel the time should be spent constructively and lead to appropriate action. To this end, therefore, we suggest that data about your portfolio be presented in a series of four tabular formats. You can do this by hand on ruled paper or you can use a computer program called "The Portfolio Monitor." (For more information concerning this program, refer to the card inserted in the back of this book.)

Tables 16.1 and 16.2 show the current status of a portfolio. The column headings indicate the stock or bond name, current price, purchase cost, your gain or loss of this moment, and whether the gains are short or long term. The summary reviews the four major categories of financial instrument, your current position in each category, and your unrealized gains or losses, both long and short term.

Table 16.1.   Current status report

Common Stocks: Name	No. of Shares	Curr Price	Curr Value	Purch Cost	Gain (Loss)	Lg Sh
Rowan	400	11.75	4,700	4,600	100	S
USSteel	500	29.25	14,625	8,100	6,525	S
Trane	100	42.50	4,250	3,000	1,250	L
Fireston	100	22.38	2,238	2,000	238	S
HewPk	100	42.00	4,200	4,000	200	S
Total			30,013	21,700	8,313	

Options: Name	Put/ Call	Strkg Price	Exp Mon	No Cntr	Curr Price	Market Value	Purch Cost	Gain (Loss)
St Ind	C	40	Feb	5	8.13	4,063	4,125	− 63
Gen El	P	55	Feb	2	4.63	925	1,030	− 105
Total						4,988	5,155	− 168

Bonds: Name	No. of Bonds	Curr Price	Curr Value	Purch Cost	Gain (Loss)	Lg Sh
ATT 1990	5	665.00	3,325	3,150	175	L
Xerox 1988	3	956.25	2,849	2,850	− 1	S
Total			6,174	6,000	174	

Mny Mkt Instru: Name	No.	Purch Date	Matur Date	Int Rate	Purch Cost
Fund	1	01/01/83	12/12/90	10.50	10,000
CD	2	10/15/83	01/15/84	9.00	5,000
Total					15,000

Table 16.2   Summary

	Current Value	Purchase Cost	Gain (Loss)	Unrealized Long Term	Short Term
Stocks	30,013	21,700	8,313	1,250	7,063
Options	4,988	5,155	− 168	−	− 168
Bonds	6,174	6,000	174	175	− 1
Mny mkt	15,000	15,000	−	−	−
Total	56,174	47,855	8,319	1,425	6,894

The distinction between short- and long-term gains is important for tax purposes. When gains or losses have been realized, that is, when the stock is sold, long-term gains are taxed at a maximum rate of 20 percent (as this is being written); short-term gains are considered ordinary income and taxed at your marginal tax rate. For many individuals this is higher than 20 percent.

Notice in Table 16.1 that the three different financial instruments are grouped and totaled separately so that you will know exactly where you stand in regard to the proportions recomended for the current stage of the business cycle.

Table 16.3 Realized gains & losses

	No. of Shares	Date Bought	Purch Cost	Date Sold	Sale Value	Gain/Loss L-T	S-T
Common Stocks:							
Hershy	500	10/14/82	14,500	11/01/83	15,750	1,250	0
Litton	100	02/15/83	5,150	06/12/83	4,850	0	−300
Total						1,250	−300

Table 16.3 shows the realized gains and losses since the start of the year. These will help you determine whether other stocks still in your portfolio should be sold and when these sales should take place. Suppose you had a large short-term profit and for other reasons are considering which of two securities to sell. If it is sold, you would take a short-term loss on the first security and a long-term gain on the second. If the sales are otherwise comparable, it would be better to take the short-term loss, which will offset some of the short-term gain previously realized and reduce your taxes. If you took the long-term gain, your tax bill would be even higher. Please note that we do not recommend that you permit tax considerations to dominate investment decisions, but clearly tax consequences should be included in your decisions.

The Current Status Report doesn't tell you whether you are exposed to more risk than is prudent, or whether a change should be made. This is the task of the other table formats. Table 16.4 shows the percentage distribution of your holdings among the investment classes and within each class.

Suppose you believe the economy is roughly half way through its expansion phase and that you now want to

Table 16.4 Distribution report

	Value	Percent	Percent
Stocks			
Rowan	4,700	15.66	
USSteel	14,625	48.73	
Trane	4,250	14.16	
Fireston	2,238	7.46	
HewPk	4,200	13.99	
	30,013	100.00	53.43
Options			
St Ind	4,063	81.45	
Gen El	925	18.55	
	4,988	100.00	8.88
Bonds			
ATT 1900	3,325	53.86	
Xerox 1988	2,849	46.14	
	6,174	100.00	10.99
Money market			
Fund	10,000	66.67	
CD	5,000	33.33	
	15,000	100.00	26.70
	56,174		100.00

hold approximately 60 percent of the total portfolio in common stocks, 20 percent in long-term bonds, and 20 percent in the money market. The Distribution Report will indicate whether you are on target.

The Distribution Report also shows the contribution that each security makes to the total value of its class. The portfolio shown in Table 16.4 has five stocks, but one of them, U.S. Steel, makes up almost 50 percent of the value of the holdings. This heavy concentration in one security should ring a warning bell. While U.S. Steel may be a fine company, its price fluctuates widely. To hold 50 percent of your common stock portfolio in one issue is dangerous. If the price should fall, the loss could swamp the gains on the rest of the portfolio for a time to come. Even if the portfolio were divided equally among the five stocks, they would each account for 20 percent of the total. This is too high. A more diversified portfolio of 15 or 20 different stocks would limit each to 5 or 6 percent of the total.

We cannot overstate the importance of diversification to successful portfolio management. Concentration gives too much importance to the individual company. If a new product fails, a new competitor enters the market, if a government contract were cancelled, or some aspect of the economy turned down, your entire portfolio could be seriously damaged.

On the other hand, when the portfolio is well diversified, the random bad fortune of one company may well be offset by the good fortune of another, and the resulting performance of the portfolio as a whole will reflect your underlying strategy rather than that of an individual company.

The format of Table 16.5 allows a quick review of the critical financial data about the companies in your

Table 16.5.   Portfolio analysis report

Stocks:	Curr Price	Curr Divid	Total Divid	Yield/ Cost	Curr P/E	High Price	Date Bought
Rowan	11.75	0.08	32.00	0.68	13.0	15.50	10/15/83
USSteel	29.25	1.00	500.00	3.42	15.0	30.50	05/15/83
Trane	42.50	1.36	136.00	3.20	17.0	47.00	11/15/82
Fireston	22.38	0.80	80.00	3.58	11.0	23.88	07/18/83
HewPk	42.00	0.18	18.00	0.43	25.0	48.25	02/23/83
			766.00	2.55			

Bonds:	Curr Value	Purch Cost	Total Intrst	Yield/ Cost
ATT 1900	3,325	3,150	168.75	5.36
Xerox 1988	2,869	2,850	315.00	11.05
		6,000	483.75	8.06

Money Market Inst:	Curr Value	Purch Cost	Total Intrst	Yield/ Cost
Fund	10,000	10,000	1,050.00	10.50
CD	5,000	5,000	450.00	9.00
		15,000	1,500.00	10.00

portfolio. The importance of dividend yield and price/earnings ratios has been discussed in earlier chapters — stocks that pay low dividends and have a high price/earnings ratio must appreciate in price if they are to provide you a reasonable return on your investment. If the price doesn't rise as expected, you could experience a substantial loss.

This table also shows the highest price reached by each stock during the last 52 weeks. This provides a reference as to how high the stock may yet go. If a stock is now at its yearly high and if its dividends are low, it may well be over-valued. Of course special circumstances can propel the stock still higher, however, when a stock approaches its yearly high it should always be scrutinized as a possible sell.

The date of purchase should always be reviewed when a stock is being considered for sale. If it is about to become a long-term gain you may want to hold it a little longer to avoid the extra taxes that would be paid. On the other hand, if you will be taking a loss on the sale you may want to sell at once since the loss will reduce your taxes on other short-term gains. If you wait until the sale is long-term, the losses must first be applied against long-term gains, which are already taxed at the lower rate.

Table 16.5 also shows the total dividend you will receive each year and the dividend yield as a percentage of your purchase cost. This will indicate whether or not you are meeting your income objective for the portfolio.

As we have indicated earlier, we recommend that portfolios be liquid (in the money market) as the economy approaches its peak, and heavily committed to stocks when it is at the bottom or beginning to rise. These tables will clearly indicate exactly what your position is at the moment so that you can judge whether and how much to move between the major instruments.

It is also important to know how your portfolio is distributed within the categories. Too heavy a concentration in a single stock or bond means that the total value of your portfolio will be tied to the fortunes of that company.

Portfolio management is a craft that can be learned. It is dependent on your skill and understanding, but it is also largely dependent on information presented promptly and readably. Take the time to build and maintain these tables and you will be rewarded with a healthy and growing portfolio.

How Money Grows

When you invest in one of the financial instruments, whether short-term instruments, long-term bonds, or equity, there are two obvious and one not-so-obvious ways the investment can grow.

1. The price of the instrument may increase over time.

2. Periodic cash payments (dividends or interest) may be paid to you, the owner.

3. The dividend or interest income received can be reinvested in the same or other instruments and can begin to earn income from numbers 1 and 2 above. Let's take a closer look at each of these using equity in a company as the instrument.

Price Changes

Stock prices change in response to supply and demand, just like apples and zucchinis. You can always look back to discover that the demand for a stock has increased by a sharp increase in the number of shares traded and the price going up. You can also always tell when the supply increased by a sharp increase in the number of shares traded and the price going down. But what causes these shifts in supply or demand?

Looking at the history of price changes in the stock won't help much. A more constructive approach is to understand the forces that truly control stock prices. These are the earning power of the company whose stock is under consideration, and the investment alternatives open to investors. If the earning power of a company (as seen by potential buyers) increases while alternative investment opportunities stay the same or become less attractive, the price of the stock will rise. If alternative investment opportunities become more attractive and the earning power of a company appears to be staying the same or deteriorating, the price of the stock will fall.

The earning power of a company can change quite quickly. When the price of gasoline escalated sharply in the late '70s the cost of operating an automobile rose. The demand for automobiles, and particularly the large gas-guzzlers, declined and the earning power of the major Detroit automakers fell. As a result their stock prices went down. When the economy began to recover and oil prices declined, people once again bought cars, even large ones. Share prices moved up.

The alternate investment opportunities open to a shareholder can also change quickly. The benchmark investment that an investor can use to measure the appeal of a given stock is a short-term interest-bearing security such as a Treasury Bill, a money market fund, or a Certificate of Deposit. If an investor can get a 14 percent return on a money market fund when a stock is returning only 10 percent, he is clearly better advised to sell the stock (thereby driving the price down) and buy Treasury Bills. The Treasury Bill not only provides a larger return, but also it is doing so at considerably less risk.

Dividends and Interest

The second way in which investments grow is through the dividends paid by common stocks and interest on bonds or short-term instruments. When a corporation earns a profit it can retain the money to invest in the business itself or it can distribute some or all of the profits to shareholders. Usually companies do a little of both.

When a company retains earnings, the money may be used to pay off debt, expand capacity, expand marketing effort, or to do whatever the management thinks will improve future earnings. The value of the company is presumed to increase and the share prices should increase. When a company distributes the earnings in the form of dividends, the shareholder has the use of these funds at once.

Different companies have different policies about

dividend payments. Small companies in high technology industries may not distribute any dividends at all. Some drug companies distribute about a third of their annual earnings. IBM regularly pays out approximately half of its earnings in the form of dividends. Utility companies often pay out three-quarters or more of their earnings.

The difference is related to the anticipated or desired growth of the company—high growth must be funded by earnings as well as increased borrowings. Investors will be attracted to those companies whose dividend policies best match their needs. Elderly or retired persons dependent on their investments for income will prefer low-risk stocks that pay high dividends. Younger investors with high current or future earning power will be more interested in companies paying little or nothing in dividends now but with the potential for considerable growth over the years.

Income on Income

The third way that money grows is when dividends or interest payments are themselves invested in the same or other financial instruments. Suppose you pay $20 per share for a stock that distributes $2 a year (10 percent of the purchase price) in dividends. You hold the stock for five years and then sell it for $40, twice what you paid. How much money did you make on this investment before taxes?

First, you earned $20 in capital gains—$40 sales price minus the $20 purchase price.

Second, you earned $10 in dividends—five yearly payments of $2. Your profit, or return, so far is $30 and the dividends represent one-third of the return. If you bought the stock only because you thought the price would increase you obviously underestimated the value.

But we are not yet finished. What did you do with the dividends you received? Suppose you reinvested them at the same rate you earned on the original $20 investment, that is, in another instrument that also pays 10 percent on the investment. Table A.1 shows how the three add up.

The $20 in capital gains represented only 62.1 percent of your total return. The $10 in dividends was 31.0 percent and the $2.21 was 6.9 percent. Put another way, if you had received no dividends at all, the stock would have

Table A.1.   Three sources of growth

End of Year	Capital Gains	Dividend	Income from Reinvesting Dividends at 10%	Total
1	0.00	2.00	0.00	2.00
2	0.00	2.00	0.20	2.20
3	0.00	2.00	0.40 + 0.02	2.42
4	0.00	2.00	0.60 + 0.06 + 0.002	2.662
5	20.00	2.00	0.80 + 0.12 + 0.008 + 0.0002	22.928
Total	20.00	10.00	2.00 + 0.20 + 0.010 + 0.0002	32.21

had to increase more than one and a half times as much as it did, in order to give you the same pretax return that you got with dividends and the return on dividends.

There are important differences among the three sources of return.

1.   The occurrence of each is not equally certain.

2.   Each return changes in response to company and economic events.

3.   The income-on-income increases over time and eventually – if you have patience – will become the most important component of your total return.

Compound Interest

Before we consider these important differences, let us take a few pages here to discuss this matter of income on income – or, more properly, compound interest – and the computer programs that have been provided in Appendix C to calculate it. In the short run, compound interest makes only a small contribution to return on investments, but if the compound interest is permitted to work for a while the results are nothing short of amazing.

Sidney Homer, author of *A History of Interest Rates* pointed out that $1,000 invested at just 8 percent for 400 years would accumulate to 23 quadrillion dollars – that's 23 followed by 15 zeros – enough to provide $5 million for every human alive. Ben Franklin was so entranced by the magic of compound interest that he left 1,000 pounds (British) to the cities of Boston and to Philadelphia. The cities were instructed to lend the money to students who would be required to pay low interest rates on the loans. At last count Boston had over $3 million in the fund even though they had already used some of the money to build the Franklin Union.

Compound interest is calculated by standard formulas so that you don't need to go through all the tedious detail of Table A.1. There are only three situations you are likely to encounter: a single payment either at the beginning or end of the compounding period; a series of equal payments over the compounding period; a series of payments of varied amount over the compounding period. You can buy a small calculator to crunch the numbers for the first two situations or, if you have a microcomputer, there are program listings in the appendix that will handle all three.

For a single payment, either at the beginning or at the end of a compounding period, there are four factors:

1.   Number of years of data, sometimes called the **term** or **maturity,**
2.   Interest rate or rate of return on the investment,
3.   Present value of this instrument, such as today's price,
4.   Future value of the instrument at the end of the term.

If you know any three of the four you can calculate the fourth. For example, if you know the number of years to maturity of a bond, the interest rate, and the future value (the face value or value at maturity), you can calculate the present value.

The single payment program asks which factor you wish to find and then for the values of the other three. For example, if you were considering buying a $10,000 face value bond that matures in five years and you wanted to be sure to earn 9.5 percent interest on the investment, how much would you have to pay for the bond today?

Given:
    Number of Years = 5
    Future Value = $10,000
    Interest Rate = 9.5
Find:
    Present Value = $6,352.28

To check this let's just work it in another way. If a five-year, $10,000 face value bond is quoted at $6,352.28 today, what is the interest you would be earning if you bought it?

Given:
    Number of Years = 5
    Future Value = $10,000
    Present Value = $6,352.28
Find:
    Interest Rate = 9.5

To repeat, if you know any three of the four factors of a single-payment investment, you can find the fourth using the single-payment program.

A slightly more complex relationship is involved when we are dealing with a number of equal annual payments rather than a single payment. We now have five factors to deal with:

1. Number of years of data, sometimes called the **term** or maturity
2. Interest rate or rate of return on the investment
3. Present value of this instrument
4. Future value of the instrument at the end of the term
5. Amount of the annual payment

In the listed annuity program only three of these five factors are needed to perform the calculation and either (or both) of the remaining two may be found. Suppose your daughter is in her senior year at high school and you want to set aside enough money today (present value) to provide $5,000 per year (annual payment) at the end of each of the next four years (term). Money-market interest rates are assumed 7.25 percent.

Given:
    Number of Years = 4
    Interest Rate = 7.25
    Annual Payment = $5,000
Find:
    Present Value = $16,840.91

Table A.2 shows how the investment of $16,840.91 at the beginning of the first year of shrinks, but continues to earn interest, as it pays out $5,000 a year for five years and ends with a balance of zero.

Table A.2.   Paying for a college education

Year	Beginning Balance	Interest Earned	Current Total	Deducted	Ending Balance
1	16,840.91	1,220.97	18,061.88	5,000.00	13,061.88
2	13,061.88	946.99	14,008.87	5,000.00	9,008.87
3	9,008.87	653.14	9,662.01	5,000.00	4,662.01
4	4,662.01	337.99	5,000.00	5,000.00	0.00

Or suppose you are about to retire and have accumulated savings of $225,000. You have invested the money in long-term bonds paying 8.2 percent and all interest will be reinvested at the same rate. For how many years of retirement could you draw $25,000 per year?

Given:
   Interest Rate = 8.20
   Annual Payment = $25,000
   Present Value = $225,000
Find:
   Number of Years = 17

Finally, let's consider a situation in which the payments are not always equal. Suppose, for example, you buy a stock today at $35 and you have been assured that the next dividend will be $2.20. You are very optimistic about the profits of this company and assume that the dividend will increase by 20 percent per year. At the end of five years you expect to be able to sell the stock for $50. What is the interest rate you will be earning on this investment? We use the internal rate of return program for this calculation which asks for the number of years and the flow of funds in or out for each year.

Given:
   Number of Years = 5
   Annual Payments =
     Start of Year 1: −35.00 (Purchase Price)
     End of Year 1:   2.20
     End of Year 2:   2.64
     End of Year 3:   3.168

End of Year 4:   3.8016

End of Year 5:   4.56192 + 50.00 (selling price)

Find:

Interest Rate = 15.22%

Note that every transaction has to be included in this analysis — including the original purchase for $35 (a negative cash flow) at the beginning of the first year, and the final sale for $50 (a positive cash flow) at the end of the fifth year. This program has to work a little harder on this problem because it is a much more complex calculation. Business managers call this the internal rate of return because it may be used to indicate the return which has been earned by a forecast stream of profits from a proposed project.

Now we can return to our consideration of how capital gains, dividends, and income on income contribute to the effectiveness of our portfolios.

Capital Gains These are the least certain source of investment growth. Stock prices fluctuate widely in time and it is not uncommon for the high price of a stock to be three or four times the low price. If you buy a stock that is out of favor (and is therefore selling at the low end of its range) and is about to come back into favor (and move towards its high price) you will be likely to make a profit on the investment.

A key to determining when a stock is at the low end of its range is to recognize that the two other sources of income — dividends and income on income — are important driving forces behind stock price changes. A stock's long-run price change is often closely correlated with its dividends because dividends are related to earning power. Dividends also prevent a stock price from falling precipitously because a lower stock price would have the effect of increasing the return percentage and the stock would attract new investors who would bid the price to or near its former value.

Stock prices may, of course, rise or fall without any important change in dividends. A price can fall when large shareholders put more shares on the market than there are people willing to buy. But this and other such temporary price aberrations are likely to be of short duration, and the average investor is not likely to be able to watch stock prices on a minute by minute schedule so as to profit by such short-term price changes.

Dividends

If a stock paid $1 in dividends in year one, $2 in year two, and $3 in year three, other things being equal, the price of the stock will rise.

If your objective is to earn a 10 percent return on your investment from dividends alone, you would be justified to pay $10 in the first year, $20 in the second year, and $30 in the third year for this stock. Moreover, investing in this stock at these prices would entail relatively little risk since the high dividend would, as we have seen, act as a support for the price.

Of course there are stocks that command a high price even though they pay only a nominal dividend. If a company earns a high rate of profit as a percent of sales, if its profits have risen steadily for a number of years, and if it can apply these profits efficiently so as to earn more profits in the future, the price of the stock will be high even if it currently pays no dividends. But these are big "ifs." If the profits of such a company falter, the price will quickly fall. A stock that pays low dividends can experience a rapid fall in price just on the basis of how expectations of, or even rumors of, future profits change. Stocks that do not pay dividends are therefore inherently unstable, volatile, and more risky than those that do.

Income on Income

This source of growth depends on the prevailing interest rate paid on reinvested dividends; and this rate depends on such broad economic factors as the pace of inflation, the level of unemployment, the size of the federal budget deficit, and many other factors.

Suppose we are in a period when interest rates are rising. A stock that pays a high dividend will be sought after because the high dividend can be reinvested at a high rate. A stock that does not pay a high dividend will be downgraded during this period because the opportunity cost of holding it is so great. During periods of rising interest rates, stocks that pay no dividends will therefore experience more sharply falling prices than those that do. During periods of falling interest rates, the opposite is true. The dividend payment is not so highly valued, and the prices of stocks that pay no dividends will tend to rise more rapidly. It is the income-on-income feature that reduces the volatility of utility stocks and others that traditionally pay high dividends.

The longer a stock is held and the higher the current dividend, the more important the income-on-income feature becomes. After five years, the income-on-income in our example amounted to $2.21 or 6.9 percent of the total return. If you held the stock for ten years instead of five, the income-on-income alone would amount to $11.874 or more than half the price of the stock when you bought it.

And the Portfolio

Income-on-income applies to the entire portfolio just as much as it does to an individual stock. To keep the income-on-income adding regularly to the total value of your investments you must continually reinvest dividends as well as the proceeds from any stock sales. This emphasizes an important difference between investment strategies.

One might be stated, "Make as much money as you can."

The other, "Lose as little as possible."

The first implies that you look to short-term capital gains as your principal source of return. You are depending on the more volatile stocks with prices that fluctuate widely in order for capital gains to be the largest, if not the only, component of your return. Typically these are stocks that pay no (or low) dividends. You must be sensitive to every rumor that comes your way and react quickly and accurately with buy and sell orders.

The second statement implies that you look to dividends and income-on-income as important components of the total return. The stock price itself is likely to change slowly, if at all, but you expect to continue to earn returns on the dividends you receive for some time.

All investments have some risk and promise some return. But the levels of risk and return are quite different depending upon the source of the return.

Risk and Return

Everyone who reads a newspaper or watches the evening news on television knows that both interest rates and stock prices can change dramatically over a short period of time. In July 1982, short-term interest rates were over 15 percent and the Dow Jones Index of stock prices was in the mid 700s. Only nine months later interest rates were 8 percent and the index was over 1200.

One implication of this volatility is that the actual return that investors receive on their portfolios is not a certain and fixed rate but rather one that changes abruptly from period to period. A thoughtful investor therefore cannot only be interested in how much he or she can possibly make, rather the investor must also be concerned with how much fluctuation will be sustained, i.e., how much risk exposure there will be.

If John cannot tolerate wide swings in portfolio returns because of personal circumstances, he should try to construct a portfolio that has a minimum of fluctuation. If Laura is in a position to bear more risk, and if she thinks she can increase her return by taking on more risk, she should construct a portfolio different from John's. Both John and Laura, however, need a framework for thinking about how much risk they are exposing themselves to and how much return they can expect as a result.

Suppose you have four possible ways to invest your money (Table B.1).

It takes no great talent to observe that Plan A offers the highest return. But that does not mean that Plan A is the way to go. What is conspicuously absent from this table is a measure of **risk**.

Table B.1. Four investments

Plan	ROI
A	22%
B	20%
C	11%
D	8%

In investment terms, risk has two dimensions — we need to know the **probability** of an occurrence and a **range** within which the probability holds. For example, your banker suggests you buy a Treasury Bill. It will cost $2,500 and will pay 7.25 percent annual interest after 90 days. That's all there is to it. You know what your investment is, you know your return, and if you believe that the U.S. government will honor its obligations, there is no doubt, no probability, hence, no risk at all in this investment. On the other hand, your sister-in-law wants to start a boutique in town and needs $2,500 to decorate the store. She says she'll pay you your $2,500 back in a year and $500 besides. That's a 20 percent return (500/2500 = 0.20) if the store does all right and your sister-in-law is the kind of person who keeps her promises. You might guess that the odds are pretty good — say nine in ten — that the store will succeed, but you have to face the fact that there is at least some uncertainty in the project, in which case the store will close and you may be out your entire $2,500. You could express this by saying there is a ninety percent chance that your return will be +20 percent, and a ten percent chance that your return will be −100 percent.

Statisticians use a chart they call a **histogram** to draw a map of the probability of an event. If each of the four proposed investments of Table B.1 were made 100 times, the statistics of the outcome in terms of return on investment might form the patterns shown in Figure B.1.

We see here that while it is true that investment A has its mean at 22 percent and investment B at 20 percent, the range of investment A is much wider than the range of investment B. That being the case, one might well choose investment B over investment A because the potential loss is less. The phrase that fund managers like to use here is that the "downside risk" of B is smaller or lower than that of A.

Risk, therefore, tells us how uncertain we are about the expected return. Another way of expressing it is given in Table B.2.

Table B.2.   Return on investment including risk

Plan	Mean Return	Chance of Occurrence				
		5%	25%	40%	25%	5%
A	22%	−8 to 4%	4 to 16%	16 to 28%	28 to 40%	40 to 52%
B	20%	5 to 11%	11 to 17%	17 to 23%	23 to 29%	29 to 35%
C	11%	6 to 8%	8 to 10%	10 to 12%	12 to 14%	14 to 16%
D	8%	− 12 to − 4%	−4 to 4%	4 to 12%	12 to 20%	20 to 28%

In words: "We estimate that there is a 40 percent chance that investment A will produce between 16 percent and 28 percent return; a 25 percent chance that it will produce between 4 percent and 16 percent or between 28 percent and 40 percent; and a 5 percent chance that it will be below 4 percent or above 40 percent."

Or, more succinctly, we can add the three center columns and say: "The odds are 90 out of a hundred that the return on investment A will be between 4 and 40 percent."

Most people feel that when the risk is high, the returns should be high—and the higher the risk the higher the returns. We expect that an investment to dig a hole in the ground will pay a much higher return, if it finds oil, than the same investment in the stock of a food company. And the investment in the food company, if the price of the stock happens to go up, will pay a higher return than an investment in a Treasury Bill. On the whole this is true. An oil gusher is less likely than a rise in the price of food stocks, and a rise in the price of food stocks is less likely than the U.S. government paying off a Treasury Bill. But it isn't always true that taking high risks leads to high returns.

There is a rather neat method of showing how different investments compare in terms of risk and reward. It is a graph on which risk and return are plotted against each other (Figure B.2). The mean or most likely return is plotted as the distance along the vertical axis. The measure of risk is the distance above and below the mean that would include 90 percent of all cases. Risk is plotted along the horizontal axis. In this way every investment is a point somewhere on the graph.

The graph is divided into four areas, each of which suggests a different risk orientation. The vertical line dividing the graph into left and right areas is drawn at what might be considered a conservative range of uncertainty—say we decide that plus or minus 5 percent is reasonable in this example. This means that in our conservative investments (plotted to the left of this line) we would expect to be 90 percent sure that our return will be within 5 percent of our predicted return. Investments plotted to the right of this line might miss the predicted return by a wider measure in 90 percent of all cases and therefore are inherently riskier.

The slanted line is drawn between two points—the point of zero risk at the left edge of the graph (7.25 percent for a Treasury Bill in this case) is one of the two. The second is the intersection of our conservative range of variability (±5 percent) with the return of an average stock. We can use a composite stock index as our measure which pays, say, 5.5 percent in dividends and another 5.5 percent in stock price appreciation for a total of 11 percent. The slanted line so determined is our **baseline.** Investments below the line are unacceptable —their return too little or are too risky; investments above and to the left are desirable—the farther above the better.

In the upper left sector we have the high-return/low-risk investments that are most desirable. These are everyone's "winners." In the lower left we have the low-return/low-risk strategies that are conservative in the truest meaning of the word—devoted to conserving our savings. They are essentially defensive. In the lower right we have the low-return/high-risk investments that are straight-out losers that offer nothing. In the upper right we have the high-return/high-risk investments that are for the high-rolling players or for those individuals with funds whose loss represents no important danger to their life style or future security.

Note that our intuition about risk and return — that higher return is achieved only by the acceptance of higher risk — is true only along the baseline. As you increase the risk by sliding to the right up the line you do, indeed, bring in a higher return. But our four investments don't all plot directly on the line. In fact, only A and C are close to the line, while B and D are quite distant — one above and one below. It turns out there are many instances in investing — and in life — like the D in this example where the risks are high and the potential return is nowhere near as high as it should be.

In this example, C is the safest choice; B is tempting for its high return; A and D offer nothing to the serious investor. One might consider a *combination* of B and C, that is, put most of the portfolio in C for assured income and growth, and a small percentage in B which would not hurt too much if it loses but could produce welcome profits if it turns out well.

Split investments of this kind make eminent good sense and here is a place where the small computer can make the job very simple. Suppose, for example, you had $100,000 to invest and wanted to split the portfolio between instruments B and C.

Table B.3. Combined risk of investments B and C

Investment B	Investment C	Most Likely Return	90% Range High	90% Range Low
100,000	0	20.0	29.0	11.0
90,000	10,000	19.1	27.2	11.0
80,000	20,000	18.2	25.4	11.0
70,000	30,000	17.3	23.6	11.0
60,000	40,000	16.4	21.9	10.9
50,000	50,000	15.5	20.2	10.8
40,000	60,000	14.6	18.6	10.6
30,000	70,000	13.7	17.1	10.3
20,000	80,000	12.8	15.8	9.8
10,000	90,000	11.9	14.7	9.1
0	100,000	11.0	14.0	8.0

A program has been provided (Appendix D) to allow you to divide a portfolio into three different instruments with different means and risk ranges. It will then produce a printout like Table B.3 to show how the proportions of investment in each instrument change the median and range of risk of the total portfolio.

Figure B.1.   Returns for four suggested investment plans show that while the means are in descending order from investment A to D, the spreads of possible returns are quite different. Choice depends on the willingness of the investor to risk a lower return or even a possible loss.

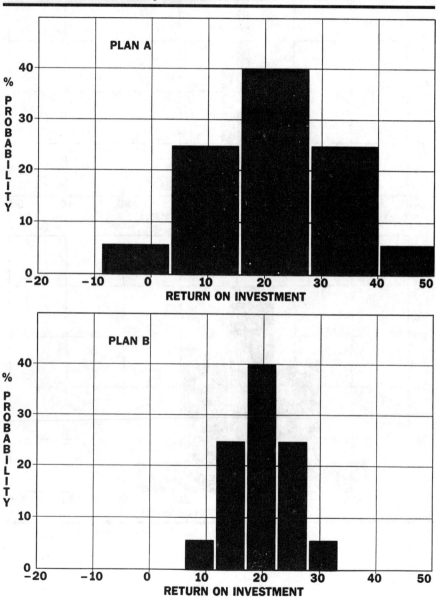

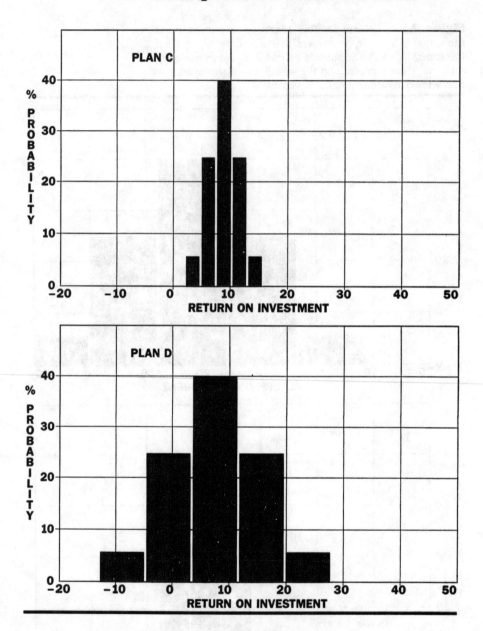

Figure B.2.   The two dimensions of risk make a map with four different territories. Risk-free return is what might be earned in a Treasury Bill or AAA-rated bond. It is, by definition, the safest possible investment. Investments that offer higher return but not much greater risk are winners. Investments that offer higher return at higher risk are for the high rollers. Investments that offer lower return at higher risk are a waste of money.

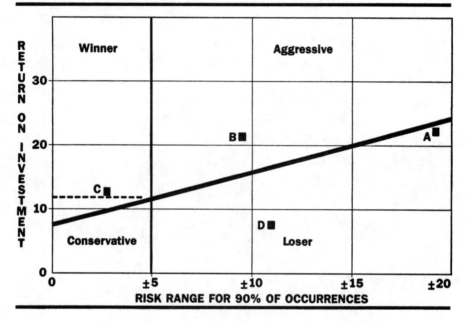

Compound Interest Program

The following program as well as those to be found in Appendices D and E have been written in a standard dialect of BASIC. We have been especially careful to avoid any special monitor control characters or other machine-specific commands so that these programs should translate easily to any computer using a reasonably standard dialect of BASIC.

The first program provides solutions for eleven compound interest equations. Nine of the eleven routines are direct solutions to the appropriate forms of the equations. Two — the interest calculation for a series of annual payments and the calculation of internal rate of return — use a trial and error technique to arrive at the solution. For these solutions the computer will go through 20 iterations in a matter of four or five seconds to come to an answer accurate to within 0.1 percent. The program is entirely menu-driven. It is only necessary to understand the meanings of the terms describing the necessary data:

Interest rate is expressed as a percent. It is the incremental value of a sum of money (the principal) kept for a period of one year. A seller of a bond pays a fixed coupon rate which, when divided by the purchase price of the bond, is the effective interest rate. The internal rate of return is the equivalent interest rate that would be necessary to provide the given flow of money over a period of years.

Number of years is the term of the investment.

Present value is an amount of money at the start of the first year of a calculation. The discounted cash flow is the present value of a future stream of yearly cash payments.

Future value is an equivalent amount of money at the end of the number years under consideration.

Payment is an amount of money paid into, or received from an investment plan. The payments may be constant for the number of years (usually called an annuity and the method used to calculate mortgages or other loans), or they may vary (as the projected earnings from a stock investment).

```
10 REM COMPOUND INTEREST
20 DIM T(20)
30 FOR J=1 TO 24 : PRINT : NEXT
40 PRINT TAB(20);"Eleven Compound Interest Computations"
50 PRINT:PRINT TAB(23);"Copyright C 1984 Richard M. Koff"
60 FOR J=1 TO 10 : PRINT : NEXT
70 FOR I=1 TO 3000 : NEXT
80 FOR J=1 TO 24 : PRINT : NEXT
90 PRINT:PRINT TAB(20);"Choose a main category by number:"
100 PRINT:PRINT TAB(20);"1  Simple Compound Interest to solve for:"
110 PRINT TAB(27);"Interest Rate"
120 PRINT TAB(27);"Number of Years"
130 PRINT TAB(27);"Present Value"
140 PRINT TAB(27);"Future Value"
150 PRINT:PRINT TAB(20);"2  Constant Yearly Payments to solve for:"
160 PRINT TAB(27);"Interest Rate"
170 PRINT TAB(27);"Number of Years"
180 PRINT TAB(27);"Yearly Payment"
190 PRINT TAB(27);"Present Value"
200 PRINT TAB(27);"Future Value"
210 PRINT:PRINT TAB(20);"3  Unequal Yearly Payments to solve for:"
220 PRINT TAB(27);"Internal Rate of Return"
230 PRINT TAB(27);"Present Value"
240 PRINT:PRINT TAB(20);"4  Return to system"
250 PRINT:PRINT TAB(27);:INPUT"Which";A$
260 IF VAL(A$)<=0 OR VAL(A$))4 THEN 80
270 FOR J=1 TO 3 : PRINT : NEXT
280 IF A$="4" THEN SYSTEM
290 ON VAL(A$) GOTO 300,390,510
300 PRINT TAB(20);"We will use Simple Compound Interest to solve for:"
310 PRINT:PRINT TAB(27);"1  Interest Rate"
320 PRINT TAB(27);"2  Number of Years"
330 PRINT TAB(27);"3  Present Value"
340 PRINT TAB(27);"4  Future Value"
350 PRINT TAB(27);"5  Return to Main Menu"
360 PRINT:PRINT TAB(30);:INPUT"Which";A$
370 IF VAL(A$)<=0 OR VAL(A$))5 THEN 300
380 ON VAL(A$) GOTO 760,840,600,680,90
390 PRINT TAB(20);"We will use the Annuity Equation to solve for:"
400 PRINT:PRINT TAB(27);"1  Interest Rate"
410 PRINT TAB(27);"2  Number of Years Using Present Value"
420 PRINT TAB(27);"3  Number of Years Using Future Value"
430 PRINT TAB(27);"4  Yearly Payment Using Present Value"
440 PRINT TAB(27);"5  Yearly Payment Using Future Value"
450 PRINT TAB(27);"6  Present Value"
460 PRINT TAB(27);"7  Future Value"
470 PRINT TAB(27);"8  Return to Main Menu"
480 PRINT:PRINT TAB(30);:INPUT"Which";A$
490 IF VAL(A$)<=0 OR VAL(A$))8 THEN 390
500 ON VAL(A$) GOTO 1080,1320,1400,1240,1480,920,1000,90
510 PRINT TAB(20);"We will use a special program to solve for:"
520 PRINT:PRINT TAB(27);"1  Internal Rate of Return"
530 PRINT TAB(32);"of a series of unequal payments"
540 PRINT TAB(27);"2  Discounted Cash Flow to find the Present Value
```

```
550 PRINT TAB(32);"of a series of unequal pyaments"
560 PRINT TAB(27);"3  Return to Main Menu"
570 PRINT:PRINT TAB(30)::INPUT"Which";A$
580 IF VAL(A$)<=0 OR VAL(A$)>3 THEN 510
590 ON VAL(A$) GOTO 1560,1860,90
600 REM*****Present Value
610 GOSUB 2080
620 PRINT:PRINT TAB(20)::INPUT"Interest Rate    :",I
630 PRINT:PRINT TAB(20)::INPUT"Number of Years  :",N
640 PRINT:PRINT TAB(20)::INPUT"Future Value     :",FV
650 PV=FV/(1+I/100)^N
660 PRINT:PRINT TAB(20)::PRINT USING"Present Value is: #####,.##";PV
670 GOTO 2060
680 REM*****Future Value
690 GOSUB 2080
700 PRINT:PRINT TAB(20)::INPUT"Interest rate    :",I
710 PRINT:PRINT TAB(20)::INPUT"Number of Years  :",N
720 PRINT:PRINT TAB(20)::INPUT"Present Value    :",PV
730 FV=PV*(1+I/100)^N
740 PRINT:PRINT TAB(20)::PRINT USING"Future Value is: ######,.##";FV
750 GOTO 2060
760 REM*****Interest
770 GOSUB 2080
780 PRINT:PRINT TAB(20)::INPUT"Number of Years  :",N
790 PRINT:PRINT TAB(20)::INPUT"Present Value    :",PV
800 PRINT:PRINT TAB(20)::INPUT"Future Value     :",FV
810 I=100*((FV/PV)^(1/N)-1)
820 PRINT:PRINT TAB(20)::PRINT USING"Interest Rate is: ####,.##X";I
830 GOTO 2060
840 REM*****Number of Years
850 GOSUB 2080
860 PRINT:PRINT TAB(20)::INPUT"Interest Rate    :",I
870 PRINT:PRINT TAB(20)::INPUT"Present Value    :",PV
880 PRINT:PRINT TAB(20)::INPUT"Future Value     :",FV
890 N=LOG(FV/PV)/LOG(1+I/100)
900 PRINT:PRINT TAB(20)::PRINT USING"Number of Years is: ####,.##";N
910 GOTO 2060
920 REM*****Present Value of Payments
930 GOSUB 2080
940 PRINT:PRINT TAB(20)::INPUT"Interest Rate    :",I
950 PRINT:PRINT TAB(20)::INPUT"Number of Years :",N
960 PRINT:PRINT TAB(20)::INPUT"Payment          :",P
970 PV=P*(1-1/(1+I/100)^N)/(I/100)
980 PRINT:PRINT TAB(20)::PRINT USING"Present Value is: ######,.##";PV
990 GOTO 2060
1000 REM*****Future Value of Payments
1010 GOSUB 2080
1020 PRINT:PRINT TAB(20)::INPUT"Interest Rate    :",I
1030 PRINT:PRINT TAB(20)::INPUT"Number of Years :",N
1040 PRINT:PRINT TAB(20)::INPUT"Payment          :",P
1050 FU=P*((1+I/100)^N-1)/(I/100)
1060 PRINT:PRINT TAB(20)::PRINT USING"Future Value is: #####,.##";FU
1070 GOTO 2060
1080 REM*****Interest Rate on Payments
```

```
1090 GOSUB 2080
1100 PRINT:PRINT TAB(20)::INPUT"Number of Years   :",N
1110 PRINT:PRINT TAB(20)::INPUT"Present Value     :",PV
1120 PRINT:PRINT TAB(20)::INPUT"Payment           :",P
1130 I=50
1140 FOR K=0 TO 20
1150 P1=0
1160 FOR J=1 TO N
1170 P1=P1+P/(1+I/100)^J
1180 NEXT J
1190 IF P1>PV THEN I=I+50/2^K
1200 IF P1<PV THEN I=I-50/2^K
1210 NEXT K
1220 PRINT:PRINT TAB(20)::PRINT USING"Interest Rate is: ####,.##X";I
1230 GOTO 2060
1240 REM*****Payments (Present Value)
1250 GOSUB 2080
1260 PRINT:PRINT TAB(20)::INPUT"Interest Rate    :",I
1270 PRINT:PRINT TAB(20)::INPUT"Number of Years  :",N
1280 PRINT:PRINT TAB(20)::INPUT"Present Value    :",PV
1290 P=PV*(I/100)/(1-1/(1+I/100)^N)
1300 PRINT:PRINT TAB(20)::PRINT USING"Payment is: ######,.##";P
1310 GOTO 2060
1320 REM*****Number of Years present value
1330 GOSUB 2080
1340 PRINT:PRINT TAB(20)::INPUT"Interest Rate    :",I
1350 PRINT:PRINT TAB(20)::INPUT"Present Value    :",PV
1360 PRINT:PRINT TAB(20)::INPUT"Payment          :",P
1370 N=LOG(1/(1-(PV/P)*(I/100)))/LOG(1+I/100)
1380 PRINT:PRINT TAB(20)::PRINT USING"Number of Years is: ####,.##";N
1390 GOTO 2060
1400 REM*****Number of Years future value
1410 GOSUB 2080
1420 PRINT:PRINT TAB(20)::INPUT"Interest Rate    :",I
1430 PRINT:PRINT TAB(20)::INPUT"Future Value     :",FV
1440 PRINT:PRINT TAB(20)::INPUT"Payment          :",P
1450 N=LOG(1+FV*(I/100)/P)/LOG(1+I/100)
1460 PRINT:PRINT TAB(20)::PRINT USING"Number of Years is: ####,.##";N
1470 GOTO 2060
1480 REM*****Payments (Future Value)
1490 GOSUB 2080
1500 PRINT:PRINT TAB(20)::INPUT"Interest Rate    :",I
1510 PRINT:PRINT TAB(20)::INPUT"Number of Years  :",N
1520 PRINT:PRINT TAB(20)::INPUT"Future Value     :",FV
1530 P=FV*(I/100)/((1+I/100)^N-1)
1540 PRINT:PRINT TAB(20)::PRINT USING"Payment is: ######,.##";P
1550 GOTO 2060
1560 REM*****Internal Rate of Return
1570 GOSUB 2080 : PRINT TAB(20);"Payments may be positive or negative."
1580 PRINT TAB(20);" If this is to find the return on an investment,"
1590 PRINT TAB(20);" the first year or two may be negative."
1600 PRINT:PRINT TAB(20);"Press RETURN when finished entering data."
1610 PRINT
1620 PRINT TAB(20)::INPUT"Payment for the beginning of year 1: ",T(0)
```

```
1630 FOR N=1 TO 20
1640 PRINT TAB(20);:PRINT USING"Payment for end of year number   ##: ";N;
1650 INPUT"",A$
1660 IF A$="" THEN 1690
1670 T(N)=VAL(A$)
1680 NEXT N
1690 PRINT:PRINT TAB(20);"We must use a trial-and-error solution."
1700 PRINT TAB(20);:INPUT"Would you like to see the successive trials (Y/N)";B$
1710 PRINT
1720 I=50
1730 FOR K=0 TO 20
1740 P1=0
1750 FOR J=0 TO N
1760 P1=P1+T(J)/(1+I/100)^J
1770 P1=P1+P0
1780 NEXT J
1790 IF P1>0 THEN I=I+50/2^K
1800 IF P1<0 THEN I=I-50/2^K
1810 IF B$<>"Y" AND B$<>"y" THEN 1830
1820 PRINT TAB(20);K+1;"th estimate is: ";I;"%"
1830 NEXT K
1840 PRINT:PRINT TAB(20);:PRINT USING"Estimated IRR is: ####.##%";I
1850 GOTO 2060
1860 REM*****Discounted Cash Flow
1870 GOSUB 2080:PRINT"We will find the present value of"
1880 PRINT TAB(20);" A stream of end-of-the-year payments."
1890 PRINT:PRINT TAB(20);"The payments may be either positive or negative."
1900 PRINT:PRINT TAB(20);"Type RETURN when finished."
1910 PRINT:PRINT TAB(20);:INPUT"Interest Rate: ",I
1920 GOSUB 2080
1930 PRINT TAB(15);" Year    Payment    Present    Cumulated"
1940 PRINT TAB(15);"                    Value    Present Value"
1950 PRINT TAB(15);"-----   -------   ----------  -------------"
1960 P2=0
1970 FOR J=1 TO 20
1980 PRINT TAB(16);
1990 PRINT USING"## ";J;
2000 INPUT"    ",A$
2010 IF A$="" THEN 80
2020 P1=VAL(A$)/(1+I/100)^J
2030 P2=P1+P2
2040 PRINT TAB(28);:PRINT USING"   #########,    #########,";P1,P2
2050 NEXT J
2060 INPUT"",A$ : GOTO 80
2070 END
2080 FOR I=1 TO 24 : PRINT : NEXT
2090 RETURN
```

Portfolio Proportions Program

This program analyzes a portfolio consisting of three instruments with different expected returns. The returns are assumed to be distributed over a range as is shown in the graph (Figure D.1). The range, and the central tendency of the range, are defined by a most likely, high end, and low end. The range should include 90 percent of all possible outcomes.

Thus the graph might be read:

Instrument I has a most likely return of 20 percent and in 90 percent of all cases, the return will never be lower than 15 percent nor higher than 30 percent.

Instrument II has a most likely return of 10 percent and in 90 percent of all cases, the return will never be lower than 7 percent nor higher than 12 percent.

Instrument III has a most likely return of 15 percent and in 90 percent of all cases, the return will never be lower than 12 percent nor higher than 19 percent.

The tables produced by the program show the combined return of all combinations of the three instruments —the most likely return, the low end of range, and the high end of range, for 90 percent of all cases— for every combination of investment in the three instruments. An example of one of the screen outputs (with instrument 3 at $60,000) is given in Table D.1.

What we are looking for is that combination of instruments which produces the maximum return with least risk. In this and the other tables produced by this program, we look for the highest "most likely" return with the narrowest spread between high and low values.

Table D.1.   Three instruments combined

#1	Instrument #2	#3	Most Likely	90% Range High	Low
0	40,000	60,000	13.0	15.5	10.8
8,000	32,000	60,000	13.8	16.4	11.7
16,000	24,000	60,000	14.6	17.5	12.5
24,000	16,000	60,000	15.4	18.8	13.2
32,000	8,000	60,000	16.2	20.2	13.8
40,000	0	60,000	17.0	21.7	14.3

Figure D.1.

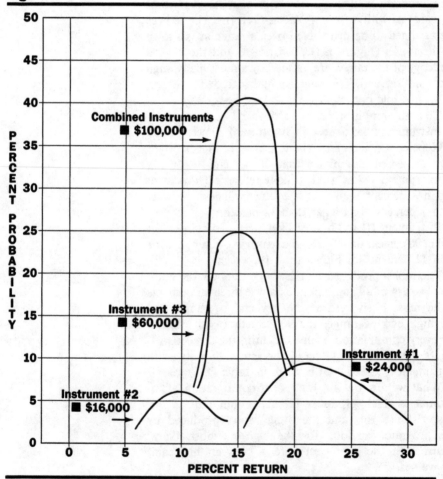

```
10 REM  THIS PROGRAM COMBINES THREE NORMAL OR SKEWED CURVES,
20 REM  IN ALL POSSIBLE PROPORTIONS.
30 FOR I=1 TO 24 : PRINT : NEXT
40 PRINT TAB(27);"A Portfolio Split Three Ways"
50 PRINT:PRINT TAB(25);"Copyright C 1984 Richard M. Koff"
60 FOR I=1 TO 10 : PRINT : NEXT
70 FOR I=1 TO 3000 : NEXT I
80 PRINT TAB(10);"This program divides three investment instruments"
90 PRINT TAB(13);"with differing return percentages"
100 PRINT TAB(13);"and differing risks associated with the returns"
110 PRINT TAB(13);"in all possible proportions."
120 PRINT:PRINT TAB(10);"It then computes the combined risk and return."
130 PRINT:PRINT TAB(10);:INPUT"Press RETURN to continue.",A$
140 A$="######## , ########, ########,  ###.# ###.# ###.#"
150 FOR I=1 TO 24 : PRINT : NEXT
160 PRINT:PRINT TAB(20);:INPUT"What is the total portfolio value? ",T
170 FOR I = 1 TO 24 : PRINT : NEXT
180 PRINT TAB(10);"You must include an estimate of returns for three instruments."
190 FOR I=1 TO 3
200 PRINT:PRINT:PRINT
210 PRINT:PRINT TAB(10);"For instrument number ";I;":"
220 PRINT:PRINT TAB(10);"What is the most likely return from this instrument";
230 INPUT R(I)
240 PRINT:PRINT TAB(10);"What are the low and high returns that will"
250 PRINT TAB(10);"bracket 90% of all possible outcomes?";
260 PRINT TAB(57);:INPUT"Low : ",L(I)
270 IF L(I)>=R(I) THEN PRINT :PRINT TAB(20);"Not low enough, please reenter.":GOTO 260
280 PRINT TAB(57);:INPUT"High: ",H(I)
290 IF H(I)<=R(I) THEN PRINT :PRINT TAB(20);"Not high enough, please reenter.":GOTO 280
300 NEXT I
310 REM  FIND MEAN and SIGMA OF COMBINATION HIGH ENDS AND LOW ENDS
320 REM  SIGMA(I) IS H(I) [OR L(I)] - M/1.645
330 FOR I=1 TO 24 : PRINT : NEXT
340 FOR K=0 TO 5
350 Q(3)=K/5
360 PRINT TAB(10);"       Instrument              90% Range"
370 PRINT TAB(10);"----------------------------- Most --------------"
380 PRINT TAB(10);"  #1      #2      #3   Likely High  Low "
390 PRINT TAB(10);"--------- --------- --------- ------ ------ ------"
400 FOR J=0 TO 5
410 Q(1)=(1-Q(3))*J/5 : Q(2)=1-Q(3)-Q(1)
420 M=0 : UH=0 : UL=0
430 FOR I=1 TO 3
440 SH(I)=(H(I)-R(I))/1.65
450 SL(I)=(R(I)-L(I))/1.65
460 M=M+Q(I)*R(I)
470 UH=UH+Q(I)^2*SH(I)^2
480 UL=UL+Q(I)^2*SL(I)^2
490 NEXT I
500 SH=SQR(UH)
510 SL=SQR(UL)
520 PRINT TAB(10);:PRINT USING A$;Q(1)*T,Q(2)*T,Q(3)*T,M,M+1.645*SH,M-1.645*SL
530 NEXT J
540 PRINT TAB(10);"--------- --------- ------ --- ------ ------ ------"
```

```
550 FOR I=1 TO 6 : PRINT : NEXT I
560 INPUT"",B$
570 NEXT K
580 END
```

Stock Sorting Program

The following program accumulates data available about publicly traded corporations and then calculates several important stock evaluation ratios including Profits/Sales, Sales/Asets, Assets/Equity, Price/Book Value, Return on Equity/Return on Comparable Investment (ROE/ROCI). Stocks are then sorted by ROE/ROCI ratio and assigned to one of four quadrants (see Figure 12.1):

1 Potential Growth Stock
2 Potential Undervalued Stock
3 Overvalued Stock
4 Candidate for New Management

```
10 REM Stock Screening Program
20 DIM A$(8,100)
30 F$="\        \ ####.## #####.## ####.# ####.# ####.# ##.### ##.###    #"
40 FOR I=1 TO 24 : PRINT : NEXT
50 PRINT TAB(35);"Stock Sort"
60 PRINT:PRINT TAB(24);"Copyright C 1984 Richard M. Koff"
70 FOR I=1 TO 2000 : NEXT
80 FOR I=1 TO 24 : PRINT : NEXT
90 PRINT:PRINT:PRINT
100 PRINT TAB(10);"This program analyzes data available from annual reports"
110 PRINT TAB(10);"and other sources about specific companies."
120 PRINT:PRINT TAB(10);"It then sorts the companies on two criteria:"
130 PRINT:PRINT TAB(15);"1. Ratio of Market Price to Book Value"
140 PRINT TAB(15);"2. Ratio of Return on Equity to
150 PRINT TAB(19);"Return on Comparable Investment"
160 PRINT:PRINT TAB(10);"Based on these criteria, stocks will fall in one of four categories:"
170 PRINT:PRINT TAB(14);" 1. Potential Growth Stocks
180 PRINT TAB(15);"2. Potential Undervalued Stocks
190 PRINT TAB(15);"3. Overvalued Stocks
200 PRINT TAB(15);"4. Candidates for Changes in Management
210 INPUT "",A$
220 FOR I=1 TO 24 : PRINT : NEXT
230 PRINT"We will need the following data about each stock:"
240 PRINT:PRINT TAB(20);"1. Company Name"
250 PRINT TAB(20);"2. Market Price Per Share"
260 PRINT TAB(20);"3. Book Value Per Share"
270 PRINT TAB(20);"4. Sales (in thousands of dollars)"
280 PRINT TAB(20);"5. Assets (in thousands of dollars)"
290 PRINT TAB(20);"6. Equity (in thousands of dollars)"
300 PRINT TAB(20);"7. Profits (in thousands of dollars)"
310 PRINT TAB(20);"8. Return on Comparable Investment (in percent)"
320 INPUT"",A$
330 FOR I=1 TO 24 : PRINT : NEXT
340 PRINT TAB(10);::INPUT"Is this a new file (Y/N)";A$
350 IF A$="Y" OR A$="y" THEN N=0 : GOTO 790
360 PRINT:PRINT TAB(10);::INPUT"What is the name of the file";N$
370 OPEN "I",#1,N$+".SRT"
380 I=0
390 WHILE NOT EOF(1)
400 I=I+1
410  FOR J=1 TO 8 : INPUT#1,A$(J,I) : NEXT
420 WEND
430 CLOSE
440 N=I
450 FOR I=1 TO 24 : PRINT : NEXT
460 PRINT:PRINT TAB(20);"Press:"
470 PRINT:PRINT TAB(20);"1. to add new entries"
480 PRINT TAB(20);"2. to correct old entries"
490 PRINT TAB(20);"3. to display table"
500 PRINT TAB(20);"4. to return to system"
510 PRINT:PRINT TAB(23);::INPUT"Which";A
520 IF A<=0 OR A>4 THEN 450
530 ON A GOTO 790,550,940,540
540 SYSTEM
```

```
550 FOR I=1 TO 24 : PRINT : NEXT
560 PRINT:PRINT TAB(21);"Press:"
570 PRINT
580 FOR I=1 TO N : PRINT TAB(20):PRINT USING"##. \      \";I,A$(1,I) : NEXT
590 PRINT:PRINT TAB(24);:INPUT"Which (press RETURN when done)";A$
600 IF A$="" THEN 450
610 A=VAL(A$)
620 IF A<=0 OR A>N THEN 550
630 CLS:FOR I=1 TO 5 : PRINT : NEXT
640 PRINT TAB(20);:PRINT USING"1. Company Name                 : \      \";A$(1,A)
650 PRINT TAB(20);:PRINT USING"2. Market Price Per Share       :$$#######,.";VAL(A$(2,A))
660 PRINT TAB(20);:PRINT USING"3. Book Value per share         :$$#######,.";VAL(A$(3,A))
670 PRINT TAB(20);:PRINT USING"4. Sales ($000)                 :$$#######,.";VAL(A$(4,A))
680 PRINT TAB(20);:PRINT USING"5. Assets ($000)                :$$#######,.";VAL(A$(5,A))
690 PRINT TAB(20);:PRINT USING"6. Equity ($000)                :$$#######,.";VAL(A$(6,A))
700 PRINT TAB(20);:PRINT USING"7. Profits ($000)               :$$#######,.";VAL(A$(7,A))
710 PRINT TAB(20);:PRINT USING"8. Return on Comparable Investment: ###.#%";VAL(A$(8,A))
720 PRINT:PRINT TAB(23);:INPUT"Which (type RETURN when done)";A$
730 IF A$="" THEN 550
740 B=VAL(A$)
750 IF B<=0 OR B>8 THEN 630
760 PRINT:PRINT TAB(20);:INPUT"Type revised data (press RETURN when done): ",A$
770 IF A$="" THEN 450
780 A$(B,A)=A$ : GOTO 630
790 FOR I=1 TO 24 : PRINT : NEXT
800 PRINT TAB(20);"Please enter the requested data about each stock:"
810 PRINT TAB(20);" (Press RETURN when done.)"
820 FOR I=N+1 TO 100
830 PRINT:PRINT TAB(20);:INPUT"Company Name (8 characters max): ",A$(1,I)
840 IF A$(1,I)="" THEN 930
850 PRINT TAB(20);:INPUT"Market Price per Share       : ",A$(2,I)
860 PRINT TAB(20);:INPUT"Book Value per share         : ",A$(3,I)
870 PRINT TAB(20);:INPUT"Sales ($000)                 : ",A$(4,I)
880 PRINT TAB(20);:INPUT"Assets ($000)                : ",A$(5,I)
890 PRINT TAB(20);:INPUT"Equity ($000)                : ",A$(6,I)
900 PRINT TAB(20);:INPUT"Profits ($000)               : ",A$(7,I)
910 PRINT TAB(20);:INPUT"Return on Comparable Investment: ",A$(8,I)
920 NEXT I
930 N=I-1
940 FOR I=1 TO N
950 T$(I)=A$(1,I)
960 T(1,I)=VAL(A$(2,I))
970 T(2,I)=VAL(A$(3,I))
980 T(3,I)=100*VAL(A$(7,I))/VAL(A$(4,I))
990 T(4,I)=100*VAL(A$(4,I))/VAL(A$(5,I))
1000 T(5,I)=100*VAL(A$(5,I))/VAL(A$(6,I))
1010 T(6,I)=VAL(A$(2,I))/VAL(A$(3,I))
1020 T(7,I)=100*VAL(A$(7,I))/VAL(A$(6,I))/VAL(A$(8,I))
1030 IF T(6,I)>=1 AND T(7,I)>=1 THEN T(8,I)=1
1040 IF T(6,I)<=1 AND T(7,I)>1 THEN T(8,I)=2
1050 IF T(6,I)>=1 AND T(7,I)<1 THEN T(8,I)=3
1060 IF T(6,I)<=1 AND T(7,I)<1 THEN T(8,I)=4
1070 NEXT I
1080 REM Sort
```

```
1090 FOR I=1 TO N-1
1100 FOR J=I TO N
1110 IF T(6,I)>T(6,J) THEN 1140
1120 SWAP T$(I),T$(J)
1130 FOR K=1 TO 8 : SWAP T(K,I),T(K,J) : NEXT
1140 NEXT J
1150 NEXT I
1160 REM sort
1170 FOR I=1 TO N-1
1180 FOR J=I TO N
1190 IF T(7,I)>T(7,J) THEN 1220
1200 SWAP T$(I),T$(J)
1210 FOR K=1 TO 8 : SWAP T(K,I),T(K,J) : NEXT
1220 NEXT J
1230 NEXT I
1240 REM Print Table
1250 FOR I=1 TO 24 : PRINT : NEXT
1260 PRINT TAB(20);"Stocks Ranked by ROE/ROCI Ratio"
1270 PRINT TAB(20);"=============================="
1280 PRINT"            $       $      X      X     X"
1290 PRINT"          Market  Book   Prof/ Sales/ Assts/ Price/ ROE/"
1300 PRINT" Stock    Price   Value  Sales Assets Equity Book   ROCI   Quad"
1310 PRINT"--------- ------- ------- ------ ------ ------ ------ ------ ------"
1320 FOR I=1 TO N
1330 IF T(7,I)<1 AND T(7,I-1)<1 THEN 1350
1340 IF T(7,I)<1 THEN PRINT
1350 PRINT USING F$;T$(I),T(1,I),T(2,I),T(3,I),T(4,I),T(5,I),T(6,I),T(7,I),T(8,I)
1360 NEXT
1370 PRINT"--------- ------- ------- ------ ------ ------ ------ ------ ------"
1380 PRINT"Quadrants are: 1--Potential Growth Stock    2--Potential Undervalued Stock"
1390 PRINT"               3--Overvalued Stock          4--Needs Change in Management"
1400 PRINT:PRINT TAB(20);:INPUT"Want to revise data (Y/N)";A$
1410 IF A$="Y" OR A$="y" THEN 550
1420 PRINT:PRINT TAB(20);:INPUT"Want to store data";A$
1430 IF A$<>"Y" AND A$<>"y" THEN 1510
1440 PRINT:PRINT TAB(20);:INPUT"Type file name (press RETURN to leave unchanged): ",A$
1450 IF A$="" THEN 1460 ELSE N$=A$
1460 OPEN "O",#1,N$+".SRT"
1470 FOR I=1 TO N
1480 FOR J=1 TO 8 : PRINT#1,A$(J,I) : NEXT J
1490 NEXT I
1500 CLOSE
1510 END
```

Index